THE RECOLLECTIONS
AND
NONSENSICAL WRITINGS
OF

A. G. CLARKE

*A
Martal Book
Publication*

Martal Book
Publications

This is a First Edition (July 2007)
ISBN 978-1-903256-37-4

DEDICATION

These nonsensical writings and references to my local Suffolk experiences have been formulated over many years.

Upon reaching the ripe old age of eighty-five, it occurred to me that other people may find interest in them, so, very belatedly I have decided to put them into print.

In doing so I would like to dedicate this work to a very good friend, The Revd John Waller, Vicar of All Saints Church, Waldringfield. He is a person of very rare qualities, having a compassionate and deep understanding of human nature and an ability to mix in society with people of all creeds, colours or politics together with a great sense of humour whilst unerringly following the teachings of his profession.

All proceeds from the sale of this book (estimated to be £1.00 per book after the production costs) will go to the local British Legion.

George and Arthur as able seamen aboard the S.S. MIRUPANU taken in 1942

INDEX

A LIFE REMEMBERED

This world in which we find ourselves helpless at our arrival and equally so on our departure is the biggest mystery of all time. It acts as a funnel and each day thousands of human beings are fed into the system and thousands are exited out. During our stay here we grow into maturity, lead our own lives n accordance with our teachings, and often are influenced by our own wishes and desires.

Apart from being registered at birth and again at death there is often no record that we have made the journey. Yet, if fortunate enough, we have spent over seventy years living out our lives. Some people are recorded in history books, some have left their mark in other ways but the vast majority vanish without a trace. It is an accepted fact that apart from the grief expressed by family and very close friends we are all more or less forgotten within a few weeks of our own demise.

We do not have to have fired a shot in anger or climbed mountains in order to have been useful to civilisation. Ordinary beings who have played their part in our community, married and produced a family; everyone has played a part and richly deserve being recorded.

Ordinary people lead extraordinary lives and those special to us are cherished parts of our personal memories. These pages recognise such a person and we hope create a lasting tribute to Arthur George Clarke.

George John Clarke an understanding and compassonate gentleman in every respect

ARTHUR GEORGE CLARKE

Arthur was wholeheartedly a country lad. He followed varied country pursuits through out his life, roaming farms and woodlands from dawn 'til dusk, always to be seen with a catapult hanging around his neck and a stout stick in his hand. He kept his Mother's pantry well stocked with game of all kinds - pheasant, partridge and rabbit and on one occasion venison. At an early age he became known as a poacher and was observed warily by all the region 's gamekeepers as a bit of a menace!

Coming from a good family background he had a wonderful opportunity in life. Arthur's father had inherited his Father's estate, which was far from wealthy. It consisted of a couple of shops in the market town of Halesworth plus a large warehouse and ten or twelve terraced houses. Years of no maintenance and neglect had reduced its value before it passed into Arthur's father's hands, who was unable to rectify the situation.

Serving as a Royal Engineer in the First World War, his Father suffered serious chest injuries whilst erecting a Bridge, which collapsed on him somewhere on the Continent. He was given only six months to live in 1916 but struggled on, departing from this mortal coil in 1955. With the death sentence he was given he also received a full disability pension. This together with the meagre rents from his property allowed him to bring up his family of six children in reasonable comfort, which in those days was quite rare. He became embroiled in local and regional politics; at the time of his death he was an Alderman of the County. He was in all respects a gentleman and did his best to instil a good standard of behaviour into his family.

The education of his son, Arthur, was very limited commencing at Blythburgh School and then on to the next village, Wenhaston. Both were council schools doing their best to ensure that all pupils left with a reasonable level of knowledge of the three 'R's'. They never produced any academics. A system was in force similar to the 11 plus and a few pupils made the grade and attended the Area School at Halesworth to complete their education.

Wenhaston School lost a promising pupil when at the age of fifteen Arthur obtained a job as a Gramophone Boy at the Empire Pool, Wembley. His work was to play records in the Pool when the resident band was taking a break and often played the Ice Skating

Stars' own particular record made to the tempo they desired to perfect their dance routine. In the case of Cecilia College he picked up a regular five-shilling tip for this which was sorely needed! On Wednesday nights he had to work over the Stadium where he operated a search light from inside the roof of the covered in area following the speedway riders around the track. (This was during the time of Bluey Wilkinson). On Friday nights he had to control the electric hare in the Stewards Box, keeping it just ahead of the dogs. All of this for twenty-five shillings a week from which he had to pay fifteen shillings lodging money. Finding things a little difficult and feeling homesick longing for the open fields and woods he asked for a rise but was refused. So he came back home to Blythburgh.

At the age of sixteen and now being quite a big strong lad he got a job for the summer pedalling a Walls Ice Cream tricycle. This was better money but as he had a few young ladies who had a liking for ice cream he found that when his books were balanced at the end of the week his finances had quite a dent in them! It was in September of 1939 when he was pedalling his tricycle around the village of Walberswick that he heard a radio near an open window stating that, as no reply had been received from Herr Hitler, we had lo consider ourselves at war. Shortly after this he volunteered for the Patrol Service in the Royal Navy giving an incorrect age to gain entry.

Cycling down to Lowestoft to report to the Patrol Service he met an old fisherman who convinced him that if he joined their crew he would earn much more money than the Patrol Service would pay. Two days later he was waiting for the bus to take him to Lowestoft to commence his fishing career. His Father, who was standing beside him as the bus stopped, leant forward and thrust something into Arthur's pocket. 'What's that for?' asked the would-be sailor. `Its your rail fare to get you home' said his Father. `You won't stick fishing for long'. The next thing though Arthur was on the Lowestoft Steam Drifter, `The Foresight', heading south for Lands End and the Bristol Channel and then on to the Irish Sea from whence the Drifter fished, selling their catch in Ballycotton and Kinsale.

By then Arthur had lost his jaunty manner and the desire to be a sailor. He had been seasick every inch of the way. Worse still, he had signed on as Ship's Cook but the thought and the sight of food was truly revolting. However, he stuck if out and the seven pounds and ten shillings given to him by his Father remained firmly safe in his jacket pocket.

This was to last only eight months, which is long enough for any human being to endure. The work was hard with very long hours; no comfort at all, no sanitation, no water except that from the Engineering Department. It was, to say the least, inhumane. Relief came when orders were received to proceed immediately to Fleetwood. Arriving there the ship was boarded at once by Naval Officials. The Navy was there in force to requisition all fishing boats for use in the Patrol Service, minesweeping, barrage balloon defence etc. Crews would be transferred with the vessel and would serve at the rank on a level with their present status. Arthur elected to opt out otherwise he would have gone full circle and ended up enlisted in the Patrol Service, which is where he was heading the morning that an old fisherman had convinced him that he could make his fortune out of a career in the fishing industry.

So, with the aid of the old steam train, he eventually reached Halesworth Station and the Eastern Counties Bus Service got him home, smelling decidedly fishy and a bit more educated in the lottery of life. After a few weeks at home - a luxury from the life aboard the fishing boat, living off roast pheasant once again - a telegram arrived from his Brother, George, saying that there was a berth for an able seaman aboard his ship, the SS Mirupanu lying in Brighton & Cowans dock in South Shields.

A reply telegram winged its way back saying that a very able seaman was already on his way to make up the crew number. Within thirty-six hours the L.N.E.R. had delivered Arthur to South Shields where George was waiting to escort him to the ship.

It was a Collier and for the next two years it plied its trade carrying thousands of tonnes of coal from the Tyne to the London Gas Depots. It was a route used by many similar ships and was known as 'E' Boat Alley. Hundreds of ships were sunk with their valuable cargo of coal, which our Industrial Depots needed badly for the gas if would produce. Every morning at daybreak the Bombers would savage the coastal convoys and every night the 'E' Boats would continue the attack. The severity of the situation can be highlighted by the fact that on one occasion when the Mirupanu sailed from Southend waters as part of a convoy of twenty-seven ships it was accompanied by two destroyers for protection. During daylight hours the convoy usually had a couple of RAF fighters giving extra cover. Only thirteen of those twenty-seven ships reached the Tyne. The Mirupanu was lucky. It survived with only one hit. Going north in thick fog the ship lost contact with the convoy. It came into a clearing with a wall of fog all around. So too did a Dormier, the pilot spotting the ship and banking round ready for the attack. Arthur had just left the fo'castle to take his turn at the helm. Halfway across the well deck he saw the pilot's face so clearly as the plane dived.

The bomb door opened and there was an almighty crash. The Ship's Gunners shot the plane down and the ship was able to limp into the Humber and up to Immingham Dock. It lay there for eleven weeks under repair before it could resume its regular trading again.

After George and Arthur left the Mirupanu they split up and joined other ships but got together again later on the Empire Ness. This ship was assigned to 'Special Services' and found itself in Southampton having minor adjustments carried out whilst being loaded with Army equipment and stores. The crew was confined to docks and no one was allowed ashore. It transpired that the invasion was on and the ship joined thousands of others anchored off the Isle of Wight waiting for the off. Not many hours later the ship was anchored off on Gold Beachhead and was being rapidly unloaded by Army personnel. Land craft and D.U.W.K.S. were being used. On the second day D+2 Arthur and his brother George decided they would like to see the Bayeaux Tapestry. They smuggled ashore in a D.U.W.K and walked off the Beachhead along a small country road.

Sounds of battle were everywhere - fighting was only a couple of miles ahead as British Troops pushed forward. As they walked along, passing Allied Soldiers addressed the two brothers in what little French language they knew. Being answered in their own tongue by two denim clad civilians somewhat astounded them! Finding the way ahead blocked by the battle, the brothers gave up the idea of getting to Bayeaux and returned to the beachhead where they discovered that getting back on board the Empire Ness was more difficult than getting ashore. Their wandering around the beachhead trying to find the D.U.W.K that had brought them ashore caused more than a few military eyebrows to be raised and they were arrested by the Beach Master, whose name

"The best mother anybody could have"

The Ancient House at Halesworth
- flagship of the 'Clarke Estate'

coincidentally was Lt. Commander A.G. Clarke! A low-key ticking off resulted but as civilians the brothers had penetrated inland occupied France some four or five miles before any other British person other than the military.

As the war moved on northward, the Empire Ness carried on taking supplies and stores up to where they were required by our forces. Home on leave, Arthur was waiting for George to telegraph details of when to return to the ship. There was a bit of a mix up and the telegram was delayed. When it arrived it advised that the ship was in Grimsby being loaded for Gent.

Arthur decided to take the train direct from Ipswich to Peterborough then across country to Grimsby. Halfway over the fens a heavy air raid occurred forcing the train to stop and dampen down its fires. Consequently, when he reached Grimsby Docks the Empire Ness was steaming away for the Continent. It made the Scheldt but was then unfortunately sunk. Every one aboard was saved but most of Arthur's possessions were still aboard, confined to Davy Jones' locker. As a punishment for missing the ship - there were no excuses as lots of seamen did this through drunkenness, marital difficulties or sheer bravado - Arthur was fined £1.00 and put aboard a small coastal vessel named The SS Cherbourg that was bound for Lowestoft.

The last ship that Arthur and his Brother sailed upon together was a small troop ship ferrying troops to and from Calais and Dover. Shortly before he undertook his last voyage Arthur was elected to represent the Merchant Navy in the Empire Festival of Youth at the Albert Hall. This entailed two weeks of practice then the actual evening performance when he marched across the Albert Hall before the King and Queen. It was a day to remember, a far cry from the days spent at Wenhaston Council School!

Home again after his last voyage, Arthur now turned his attention to getting a job. He thought he had made it when he signed on for long shore boat fishing off Southwold Beach His Skipper and the boat owner was Andy Palmer. They managed to get off the beach and laid out the long lines for Cod and Whiting but the weather blew up very rough It was a very long two or three weeks before the weather settled enough for them to get off and haul their lines. It was a good catch but all the fish on the hooks had drowned and had to be thrown back into the sea. Adverse weather prevailed that winter and Arthur earned very little from long shore fishing.

He decided to change jobs and managed to secure a position at Southwold Gasworks. This was a small gas company owned by George Crick. Taking Arthur into the gasworks, George asked one of the stokers to top up one of the re-torts. Arthur stood and watched. The stoker opened up the next re-tort, handed Arthur the shovel and said 'Have a try'. Jacket off, Arthur's first shovel of coal hit the back of the retort and he filled it up to the front as it should be. George Crick said 'You've done this before!' Arthur nodded - he had stoked ships at sea when a stoker had been taken ill and they were much bigger furnaces than those at the Gasworks. So he became a full-blown stoker immediately. He had initially been taken on as a trainee at about two-thirds pay on an eight-week probation basis. The second night of working there, he was asked to do the night shift having been shown how to operate the valves of the single gasholder, a task that he completed with no bother. The end off the week was payday. Going into the office, George paid him a trainee's wage. Arthur disputed this thinking and requested a full stoker's pay having carried out all of the work with no training and with no trouble. The owner of the Gas Company refused so Arthur collected his bicycle and was off.

The next job he found was one working with a gang of itinerant Irishmen who travelled from farm to farm carrying out seasonal work such as haymaking, harvesting crops, cutting edges and digging ditches lo assist land drainage and threshing corn stacks in the winter months. There was always work for them and they were much in demand. All of the work they did was priced - no day work rates applied. Consequently, when farm wages were just under five pounds per week, Arthur and his Irish colleagues were earning twenty pounds. It was about this time that Arthur made a vow. He vowed that he would retire at the age of fifty and that he would own a Rolls Royce when he did so. As it would transpire he would indeed drive a Rolls Royce but he has never fully retired! Working with the Irishmen gave him the idea of starting a labour supply company on a proper basis and before long he was employing twenty-seven men going from farm to farm. Digging out a ditch one day he came across a tree stump, which had grown from the hedgerow and blocked the ditch. It took all day for him to chip away at it and clear a passage for the water to get away. That night he wrote to I.C.I. and asked for information on the use and storage of explosives. Within a couple of weeks he had police

permission to store and use gelignite and some good advice on
how to use it.

Shortly after that he had an expanding business removing tree
stumps. Farms were being converted into bigger fields and
agriculture was changing rapidly. He had two or three old vehicles
that were used to take the men lo work. A new vehicle had been
ordered and he had it sign-written with the words 'Blast That
Stump'. It was a winner and for many years he became known as
Blast That Stump, and still is amongst the older generation today.
The war had created many thick concrete structures around the
fields and on the coastline. Arthur found himself contracted to the
War Office to remove these structures. It was easy with explosives
and before long he entered the field of general demolition.
Agricultural work was being dropped off gradually and the work
of Civil Engineering was embraced more and more. It was around
this time 1947-1950 that he hired his first farm, The Red House at
Frostenden. It gave shelter to the vehicles and machinery that had
been acquired for the demolition work. There was also room to
start a one hundred sow pig-breeding unit. Within two years, he
had bought not only The Red House Farm but also the Red Cap
Farm in Hinton. More pigs were produced at the Red Cap Farm
and a herd of cows were purchased with the Red House Farm. It
transpired however that farming was not to be a success for Arthur.
Looking back it was obvious that he had over reached and did not
have the farming knowledge that was essential for success. Both
farms were placed on the market and sold off leaving a sum of
money that was injected into the demolition business.

As the demolition business grew another side was emerging, that
of landscaping and grounds maintenance for the Ministry of
Defence. The company was contracted to maintain many of the
local airfields and military bases. In the last years of the Cold War
the company maintained six military bases for the British Army of
the Rhine in Germany. Arthur's family now operate the businesses
on a much sounder footing and both have become well known
throughout the country for the work they have done. Quite
recently, someone who juggles statistics rated CDG Demolition
Ltd as number two Hundred in the world.

Arthur has had a full life and lived well off his earnings. Now in
his eighty-first year he enjoys reasonable health and still enjoys the
family businesses - albeit from a distance!

STANDING UP WELL

During one's lifetime it is almost inevitable that what one does - at the time we regard it as an everyday experience, something we do in the course of a day's work - will appear in fifty years as a piece of history or considered a most unusual occurrence. Thus I came to realise that some fifty years ago I was fortunate to be able to participate in such an occurrence. Indeed, at that time, had the McWhirter brothers launched their Guinness Book of Records, I really believe that I would have achieved a level of fame.

Perhaps one of my failings is that I have never religiously kept a diary of the course of time during my life and then, after half a century, it is most difficult to bring past event clearly into focus. However, the incident to which I refer took place in the mid fifties - probably about 1956. I had by that time been out of the Merchant Navy for some ten years and had chosen to be self-employed. Whilst having no working experience in the use of explosives or any mental knowledge or learning of this dangerous substance, I had foreseen the invaluable use of this product in reforming the country's agricultural policies and where farmers would no longer find it economical to cultivate and crop small and irregular shape fields.

The need to remove hedgerows and hedgerow trees would arise to create large fields of up to 500 acres and more. What better way could there be of removing a large oak tree stump of perhaps two tons in weight and five feet in diameter than a strategically placed charge of explosive right under it's backside and lifting it, shattered but in manageable sections out of the ground where it commenced life as a small acorn perhaps a century and a half ago!

Fortunately for me my local police department thought I was sound and stable enough to hand and store explosives. With this - and the assistance of a couple of handbooks from the ICI Explosives Division - I found myself in business. As anyone could well imagine - using explosives as I did in the course of time throughout East Anglia and well beyond it's boundaries - many incidents would arise which were well worth recording. Perhaps they may well make another story.

The incident, which I am now coming to, was perhaps my one

and only chance of getting into the Guinness Book of Records. It took place at South Cove near Cove Hythe, which is on the coastline some two or three miles east of Wrentham - a small village on the A12 a few miles south of the port of Lowestoft. Should any reader be young enough not to have shuffled off this mortal coil, they may well remember that South Cove and Cove Hythe were sites chosen by the Ministry of Defense as being strategic for the protection of the east coast from any invading enemy. Gun emplacements were constructed, cliff top lookout posts and scores of timber army huts erected to house the vast numbers of military personnel which would be required to man the defenses. It must be remembered that way back in 1914, country areas such as South Cove had no supply of piped water therefore many wells had to be sunk which were the only supply of water the army had. The water table around that area was about 65-70 feet.

We will recall that after the First World War, history repeated itself in 1939 and once again the MoD visited Sir Thomas Gooch's estate and put requisition orders on the land behind the cliff top at South Cove and Cove Hythe. Again heavy artillery was placed pointing out across the North Sea. However, on this second occasion no dependence had to be placed on deep wells - piped water was then available and the Second World War was played out in comparative comfort - that is, of course, just the part that was played from the cliff top at Cove Hythe and South Cove.

On both occasions, 1914 and 1939, the area of land occupied by our troops was well inland - probably a 1000 yards or so inland from the sea. The North Sea is known to be vicious and when its temper is aroused the raging sea is prone to claim may yards of our coastline each year. I do not have any statistics of this or know of any that exist but it is a certainty that by now all the land which was used by the military authority during both wars is now well and truly under the North Sea.

So this brings me back to 1956 when after a particularly wild and stormy night, I received a telephone call in the morning from Mr. Walker, Estate Manager for Sir Thomas Gooch. He was strangely secretive and said he had an urgent task for me to carry out. He did not enlighten me as to what this was but would I pick him up at the Estate Office, which stood on the side of the A12, a mile south of Wrentham, and bring my explosive gear and explosives with me? So I set out to do his bidding.

He climbed into my Dormobile van and directed me to drive to South Cove. The road was a dead end and ended on the cliff edge. Getting out of the van we walked to the cliff edge and there, some 50 or 60 feet below, on the beach, stood what looked very much like a roughly constructed factory chimney. The North Sea had yet again claimed several yards of coastline and what I was seeing standing upright on the beach was in fact one of the 1914, 65 ft wells - now represented as a 65 ft brick tower! How the sea had managed to wash right round the structure and leave it standing was a complete mystery. Perhaps it is a recommendation of the workmanship of the Well Sinker who built it in the reverse order - as a well.

It was, of course, now a danger to anyone who attempted to climb it or even stand too close. Within a few minutes I had laid it flat. Within those few minutes did I make history? Is there anyone out there who has shared the same experience? Would I rate as the only person ever to have `blown up' a 65 ft deep well - or did I blow it down?

CONVERSATION OVERHEARD

The conversation which I heard
Could be repeated - word for word.
With confidence - if I knew
That what I heard was really true.

For all too often, words are said
Which have no real foundation,
But from them other rumours spread
And so does condemnation!

So who should really take the blame
If idle talk condemns a name!
No one knows who had the say
When an informant says its "They".

It would appear that what "they" say,
Leaves no doubt that it must be right.
But to me its neither black or white –
And is indeed a shade of grey.

Such talk is passed from mouth to mouth
From East to West and North to South.
And oft - at stages, the message sent
Gets added to, for embellishment.

So next when idle talk prevails
Far better to use discretion.
And when a wagging tongue assails –
What you hear you will never mention!

A WOMAN, A DOG AND A WALNUT TREE

There are of course many different types of these species all round and it could be considered that the old folk-lore sayings could be unfair to some, if applied in general terms. It could not possibly relate to all Women - all Dogs or all Walnut Trees!

To the uneducated - or perhaps to those not fortunate enough to be born in Suffolk or Norfolk - I ought to explain that it has always been a well-founded belief that as the saying goes, "A Woman, a Dog and a Walnut Tree - the more you thrash them the better they be!" Mind you, having lived in Suffolk all my life I have never met or heard of anyone who has applied any measure of corporal punishment on all three and lived to boast of his achievement - or even had the temerity to admit to such practices. Yet constantly throughout my allotted span of life I have heard the old saying repeated many, many times, and without doubt at some time or other some 'owd Suffolk Boy' has done so and kept very quiet about it.

Now I have to admit that I have been guilty along these lines to some measure or degrees. Having enjoyed - endured - suffered or tolerated a marriage for some years now, battered and buffeted by considerable turbulence through those years, the old Suffolk saying has been ringing in my ears and I have looked at my Wife and given serious consideration to the improvements which could possibly be achieved by applying the measures recommended.

Of course it does not necessarily imply that all females at the receiving end of these measures has to be you Wife! Indeed, it could be that the treatment recommended would be much better bestowed on another man's Wife, or perhaps a high-spirited Spinster?

Unless one had very close knowledge of a woman's failings it would be most difficult to adjudicate whether or not any improvements could be achieved by applying these remedial measures.

Pondering over this for some time I considered that my judgement might be somewhat biased and on that score I decided not to proceed to put the first option into practice! So I turned to the second option - my dog. She is a black smooth coated Retriever of just over a year old. She and I share our time together on most days and we have developed a perfect understanding. She is fully aware that I would not hurt a hair on her body and she has almost unlimited license to ignore my requests or instructions and turn a completely deaf ear to my whistle when I call her to heel. After all, she knows that what she is doing is most enjoyable and not really offending anyone - so why should she answer to my bidding?

Most mornings we walk over the Golf Course where we have a couple of ponds, and Meesha - that's her name - very much enjoys a swim. On the occasions - and there have been many - that she dashes up on to the Green and snaffles a ball that an ardent Golfer is just about to putt for a Birdie, I have been quite annoyed with her. On one occasion when a four-ball game was in play, she nipped in quickly and snaffled all four balls in one mouthful! Fortunately the Golfers, who all love her, could see the funny side of the episode and as they were not in contention for a Silver Cup, or playing for a row of houses, no harsh words were said.

However, I remembered the second option and did tap her rear quarters very lightly with my walking stick, where upon she rolled over on her back with her paws in the air (most unladylike), but as always her eyes full of mischief which would melt the hardest of hearts, so as you can imagine, I was very easily led into abandoning my second option.

So I turned my thoughts to my third option. This was easy! Twenty-five years ago I planted three Walnut trees in my garden and have watched them grow into sturdy trees of nearly thirty feet tall. Each year as they matured I have talked to them; have cajoled them; and even threatened them - but up to last year they have completely failed me. In a joint effort last year they managed to produce just ten walnuts. I searched each bough to find them, and even then my uncompromising trees grew them where I could not reach. So I let them know of my displeasure and when the time came to gather my meagre harvest I found a long pole to dislodge the ten nuts, which I had seen and counted - all to no avail. The Walnut trees had the last laugh. The Grey Squirrels had got there first and the cupboard was bare!

Now most men would agree that such blatant and complete disregard and open confrontation would test any man's patience, and mine was no exception. So I warned my trees that they had their last chance to make amends, and having failed, they were now in for it in a big way. I would now put option three into practice. Having hardened my heart to any pain and suffering those poor trees might endure, I got a very heavy ball-point hammer and explained to the trees that had they tried to be just a little more industrious in the past, this would never have happened. As I did so, I lambasted the trunk with my hammer, many times, and left them all severely bruised and battered. Their wounds still show to this day and will forever be visible. However, option three worked most successfully! This year, the first time ever, my three Walnut trees are laden with young walnuts. A mouth-watering sight to behold and even if the grey squirrels who stole last years crop return will all their relations to thieve yet again, there will still be plenty of nuts for me.

Perhaps I should amend that, and say "us", because my Wife enjoys a wet walnut just as much as I do, and because I decided not to put the first option into practice, we are still married. And no doubt because I decided also not to put the second option into practice, Meesha will sit in her bed beside the radiator and watch us enjoying some wet walnuts with a glass of port during the evenings.

Now as I walk past my recently faithful Walnut trees, I sense that they now regard me with some reverence and that I will never again need to chastise them. But I am left wondering about the first and second options, and will never really know the answer!

THE LIGHTHOUSE

These lights have shone for many years
Calming nerves, removing fears
Providing hope, with hearts to ease
For all the men who sail the seas.
Around our shores they stand, windswept
On highland and on headland
The lonely vigil, nightly kept
As ships sail on while sailors slept.
Throughout the night
Their shafts of light
Rotate in well-timed motion
Signposts of the sea are they
Guiding ships across the ocean.
From Flamboro' Head - sail on your way
South, to the light of Whitby Bay.
Voyage on across the bight
Until you see the Happisburg Light
Then across Sole Bay where can be seen
The welcome light of the Southwold Beam
Southerly still, the shore caress
The light appears at Orfordness
When the vessel berths
And the voyage is o'er
Give thought to the light
That from the shore
Cast it's beam that sailors might –
Soundly sleep on the darkest night,
To complete their journey, strong and brave
Fearing not an ocean grave.

THE BROODY HEN

During the transition of time - village life has produced many characters. One such village, Wenhaston near Halesworth, has had its fair share of these people.

This short story happened way back - in the days when every household in the village kept a few chickens - fed on household scraps mostly. Each year the men of the village would put down one or two `settings' of eggs to hatch off and provide new young stock for egg production and cockerels for the table at Christmas and Easter. `Settings' of eggs - thirteen in number - would exchange ownership for little more that the cost of a dozen eggs for consumption. These `settings' would have to be obtained from a source where a cockerel roamed free with the chickens thus ensuring that the eggs were fertile.

Nature, over the course of time, has also ensured that chickens - after the Spring flush of eggs - would become `broody and there were no forces of nature which could prevent a broody hen from contentedly ruffling her feathers and sitting down for a long three weeks over a clutch of eggs to incubate them. When well into the period of incubation, the owner would happily observe that she was `sitting tight'.

However, as in all aspects of nature, sometimes the `norm' would not materialise and the unfortunate householder who needed to replace his laying stock for the following year, did not have a broody hen. Help was always at hand and another villager would be pleased to lend a broody hen as a surrogate mother. After incubation had taken place and the young chicks fully feathered, the hen would be returned to its rightful owner. No payment would be asked for - the owner had been relieved of feeding the hen over a period of nearly twelve weeks, which was ample reward.

Sam - now long since moved on to pastures new - was asked if he had a broody hen by a friend who lived on Blackheath. `Why yes!' replied Sam - I've got two or three getting quite broody. I will bring you one.

Three days later Sam and his wife were going out in the evening. Sam did not drive but some kind friend had picked them up. Sam sat in the front of the car and his wife got in the back. Approaching the Star Inn, Sam - who had completely forgotten his promise to lend a broody hen – asked the driver to stop whilst he got some cigarettes. Entering the bar to get his fags, Sam was surprised to see his friend sitting there.

`Did you bring the old hen?' he asked Sam.

A little perplexed, Sam said `Yes, as a matter of fact I did - she's in the back of the car!'

DID YOU SEE THAT?

Whilst we are soundly and safely tucked up in our beds, strange things are happening in the nocturnal hours all around us. Travellers in cars often report seeing an unusual animal as their car headlights sweep the countryside. For some reason these animals are always thought to be black and greatly resemble a panther. Nobody, it appears, has yet seen anything resembling an elephant or a giraffe in the wild. National reports of sightings of a mysterious black dog-like creature have become quite commonplace, often being supported by local farmers who have discovered some of their cattle and sheep badly mauled and ravaged - obviously by some carnivorous creature. Nobody has any clue to their origins - theory has it that they were once small cuddly pets turned out into the wild and as they grew to maturity they displayed their natural aggressiveness. Not many years ago a black panther-like creature was spotted several times in the neighbourhood of Shooters Hill, London. Daily newspapers made a meal of the story for several weeks and more recently we have the `Beast of Bodmin' in our midst supported by a rather indistinct photograph taken by an amateur photographer. Again, very recently, we have reports of further sightings of a similar creature seen more than once on the fringe of Thetford Forest. Only days ago another reported sighting of a black panther-like creature just north of Saxmundham generated much interest and speculation. Obviously there must be very many of these strange creatures roaming around the country - there are far to many sightings now over an area of many counties for there to be just one or two of these animals at large. So what's new? Ask any East Anglian if he knows who or what `Black Shuck' was! Many will probably guess and answer by saying that it is an illegal immigrant discovered in a container at Felixstowe Dock but some will know that `Black Shuck' is probably the most notorious wild panther-like creature ever to have been confronted - not just a sighting but a real encounter where the creature has appeared in our midst and left its mauled victims on display for all to see. The reason that I write this tale is because I fully believe that `Black Shuck' - be it in a ghostly form or in the flesh - still roams our Suffolk villages as will become clear as this story goes on. First let me give a brief history of what is known about `Black

Shuck'. An authentic report in local history tells us that the creature appeared in 1577 and entered the church at Bungay, Suffolk whilst the congregation was at prayer. As it tore through the pews it killed two people and severely injured a third, witnessed by the entire congregation - there was no doubt whatsoever. A parishioner, who was in the congregation, one Abraham Fleming who later took the Cloth and became a rector in London, was able to vividly describe the creature in a book which he published later. His report says that the animal emitted fearful flashes of fire and travelled with incredible haste. He further relates that the injured person was badly burnt by the heat, which the animal generated and that the skin on his back was shrivelled and resembled leather. This incident was of sufficient substance to incite the locals to erect a weather vane in the market place depicting the animal. It remains there to this day. Very shortly after this the beast repeated the performance in the village of Blythburgh - which happens to be where I was born. This time it entered the church and secreted itself on a beam or shelf. As soon as the congregation bowed their heads in prayer, it leapt down from its hiding place and tore through the pews, quickly dispatching two men and a lad, severely burning the hand of another man and "blasted" many more who were close by. Before it left the church it lunged at a heavy oak door and left its fang marks scored deep in the oak. Again this was not just a `sighting'. Three more corpses and several injured worshippers supported this horrific confrontation with the ferocious creature. Who could disbelieve these strange occurrences when the deeply scored fang marks on the heavy oak door in Blythburgh church still remain there for all to see after a period of more than 400 years has elapsed. Even the strongest critic would be hard put and find great difficulty to argue against all these facts, which after all, are well recorded in the archives of local history. Not just sightings which could be somewhat illus ional, depending of course, on whether the informant of the incident had spent a quiet hour or two in The Red Lion beforehand. So I confess that I am a strong believer in the former existence of `Black Shuck' and through my acquaintance with a good friend named Henry, my belief is unshakeable that it does indeed still exist. Perhaps now is the time when you should re-charge your glass and settle down comfortably whilst I relate my story.

I quite forget when I first met Henry. It was through a mutual acquaintance, but how and when our paths first crossed escapes my memory. After all, age is settled in with both of us and we can be forgiven for the odd blank times in our memories. It was probably nearly twenty years ago. Henry is a likeable fellow - happily married with a grown-up family. Quite typical of any good, honest, law-abiding man approaching his allotted span of life. He is the type who is always first to put his hand into his pocket and is more than willing to buy a round of drinks. Mind you, he is not rich by any standards, just retired on a pension and with what he and Betty have managed to save over the years. Like very many others, he decided to leave town and retire to the country and has managed to do so by selling his town house well and buying a country property very wisely, creaming off a little tax free capital to augment his savings and make retirement a little more comfortable. Just what you would expect him to do. I would slot Henry into the category where he would not stand out in a crowd. After all, he cannot muster many inches above 5 ft in height. He has never boasted of any extraordinary exploits or achievements, although now and again a twinkle enters his eye as he remembers his youth. He is one of many thousands of men who would slot into the category "A good citizen". Solid and sound in every respect. He speaks ill of no fellow man; would help anyone in trouble and do so willingly. Giving is far more pleasurable than receiving. You know - the sort of chap with whom you would willingly share trouble with, or accept as a companion if marooned on a desert island.

Quite recently - perhaps two years ago - Henry decided that his neat and spacious bungalow at Wickham Market, with its equally neat and tidy garden, would benefit greatly by having a fishpond installed. Just the sort of thing you would expect him to want. He gets great delight in feeding the fish and attending to their needs before he gets out his deck-chair and fondly watching them swimming around. Not an unusual pastime and pleasure for a man of his years. This winter he decided that the fishpond needed a good spring clean. So having found a suitable receptacle to house the fish during the cleaning operation, he approached the pond with net in hand, filled with quiet confidence. Then he fell in. There is nothing unusual about that, it's just the sort of misfortune that one would normally expect to befall Henry.

Neither would you expect him to relate such an unfortunate occurrence to his friends. He didn't -but his wife did. So we all had a jolly good chuckle and Henry joined in, just as you would expect him to do. In the early days of our friendship, he and Betty lived on the outskirts of London, on the east side, quite near Romford. For some years I did not get to know just how he earned his living, but I now discover that he managed a stock-broking company in the City. This is quite foreign to his image, being such a quiet and peaceful type of fellow, the hurly-burly of high finance and the fast wheeling dealing of the City does not seem a bit like Henry. Anyone could be forgiven for thinking him to be running the small corner shop and extending credit whenever difficult times existed. Betty worked too, after their family had grown and fled the nest.

Henry always looked forward to his retirement, mainly because he enjoys a game of golf. He is not bad at it, always playing a good game, even if it is off a doubtful handicap. Whilst in Romford he played an active part in fund-raising for the local Royal Air Force Association - just the sort of thing you would expect him to do. He was, I understand, Chairman of the local branch. It was only quite recently that I learnt of the reason for his great love and loyalty to the RAF. Believe it or not, this quiet genial little fellow was born with a heart strong enough to hurtle a Spitfire fighter plane through the skies. He was not one of `The Few', those dauntless young men who kept our British skies free of enemy aircraft. He did not spend his time circling the heavens to find the Red Baron, as did Douglas Bader and Johnny Johnson. Henry had an equally hazardous task in flying with the famous 702 Squadron, protecting our forces from marauding aircraft in the Middle East. Looking at him now as he plays a round of golf, it is most difficult to relate him with flying anything more dangerous than a kite on the end of a length of twine - yet alone a Spitfire powered by Merlin engines with over a thousand horse power! But that's just what he did. Should he ever have been invited to appear on the TV panel game with Gilbert Harding, I am sure that no-one would ever have guessed his secret. Secret it is - because as I have said, Henry never boasts of his past endeavours. However, that was very many years ago, and we who enjoy and share his company at the Golf Club are oblivious of any rank or position, which he may once have proudly held. So

we have, affectionately of course, bestowed the rank of
"Corporal" on him. He offers no objection and responds to this
in his normal, quiet and unassuming manner. Travelling to his
office in the City and bringing up his family on the
outskirts of the Metropolis, I very much doubt if Henry ever
dreamed that one day he would be living out his retirement in
the heart of rural Suffolk, where once the self-appointed
"Witchhunter General" ran amok in the late sixteenth century,
persecuting any poor old widow who was unfortunate enough
to harbour a black cat, ensuring that his henchmen earmarked
them as candidates for the Ducking Stool or for Burning at the
Stake; and where country folk were once terrorised by an
enormous black dog-like creature, known as `Black Shuck'
which would leave all its victims lifeless with terrible injuries to
their throats where its fangs had sunk in deep.
Being such a kindly person it was just as well that Henry knew
nothing of these violent incidents, which once happened
throughout Suffolk so many years ago. But move to Suffolk he
did, and happily settled down in the peace and quiet of
Wickham Market. He had chosen well, his bungalow sported a
real live fireplace where a large fire grate held half a dozen
good-sized logs. Henry and an open fire could not possibly be
thought of apart. Meeting Henry for the first time, warmth,
comfort, serenity are immediately conjured up in ones mind. Not
to mention Henry's love of food. He is very partial to roast
chestnuts, which when in season, give him immense pleasure.
Sitting in front of their new-found fireplace - the logs crackling
away merrily, Betty and Henry would enjoy these delights. It
was a rather wild night soon after they had moved to Suffolk
when, as winter's darkness fell, Henry eased himself out of his
armchair, drew the curtains across the windows and threw more
logs on the fire. At peace with the world, his mind wandered
ahead and he thought of the month of March. By the time
March has arrived with its fine carpets of snowdrops, as the
month wore on the daffodils would appear and nod lazily in the
breeze. He liked the thought of March and the approaching
Spring weather, It meant that he could enjoy playing golf more
and that his thermal underwear could be put away for another
year. Lying back in his armchair with these pleasant thoughts
running through his mind he was almost comatose in the comfort

and warmth, which surrounded him. Betty had nodded off beside him when he suddenly became aware of a noise outside his front door. Again his raised himself from the armchair and made his way to the door. They were not expecting any friends to call on such a wild winters night. Opening the door he stood for a few seconds transfixed. There on the doorstep stood an enormous Black Dog - the size of which he had never seen before. Its eyes glowed red in the darkness, its lips were curled back and its fangs were bared. Terrified for the first time in his life Henry slammed the door shut and retreated to the safety of his armchair. He was badly shaken and needed a large Brandy. His heart beat rapidly. Had he been dreaming - did he really see this enormous, ferocious looking, black dog? At the back of his mind he knew.

It was a day or two after, whilst we were chatting over a drink, when he timidly ventured to relate the story to me. He quite expected me to erupt in volumes of laughter, which would be my normal reaction. Not on this occasion. I knew too - Henry was probably the first person for more than three hundred years to come face to face with `Black Shuck' - and without doubt, the only person ever to do so and live to tell the tale.

One, Two, Three
Mother caught a flea
She put it in the teapot
And made a cup of tea!

This rather nonsensical little nursery rhyme no doubt has been chanted by millions of children throughout the century, probably by reason of the fact that fleas (SIPHONAPTERA) and we humans (HOMO-SAPIENS) often had a shared existence. In many cases the relationship went further and we often became bedfellows! Of course that was in the days before we humans has achieved the high standard of hygiene as is enjoyed today. There were no insecticides then - no aerosol sprays, which now eradicate insects by the thousands with just one jet of spray.

My dear old mother developed such a hatred of fleas that upon the very utterance of the name - let alone the sight of one - she would instantly change from her normal kind-hearted, generous, forgiving self into a kind of demonic irrational creature. Though never a highly religious person, she could see no reason why fleas were ever given the right to be in this world and that this was a complete indiscretion of the Great Architect of the Universe and for which she could never forgave Him.

I firmly believe that she had a sort of sixth sense over fleas, she could almost hear the little blighters creeping around. Woe betide any flea which dared to cross her threshold. Inevitable, of course, they did manage to gain entry into the house - I hasten to say not in great numbers - more often than not it was just a single nomadic creature that appeared in her normally spotless household and what a turmoil it created! To give shelter, unknowingly or unwittingly, to a common flea was a stigma - a blot on the family name, so to speak, and when it did happen not a word of it should be breathed outside the house and we were, as small children, sworn to secrecy. One never really knew how such an insignificant little thing as a flea ever found its way through the door. Mother had her idea of its origin - such as an occasion when she had been up the village shopping and she remembered that she had brushed against that Mrs …………who lived in the Farm Cottages, whilst she was in the shop. `That's it for sure!' she would expostulate - `I always did think she never looked very clean.' The poor woman was probably completely innocent of the charge but as I have said, where a flea is concerned, Mother became completely irrational.

I remember one occasion she returned home from a shopping trip looking decidedly uncomfortable having an occasional scratch here and there. Then she announced it! `I think, ' she said in very chilling words, `I've got a flea. ' At this, the whole household went on instant red alert. We all knew our duty in such emergencies and stood by our action stations. Peering down inside her blouse she searched for the offending insect. Father was allowed to assist but only as far as the bounds of decency would allow. Then came the first sighting. The cunning little insect projected itself off her person in the same manner as a fighter plane off the deck of the Ark Royal.

The family had already taken up their battle stations and all eyes were peeled to spot the flea when it next appeared. I did say that Mother had an extraordinary sense about fleas and wearing a very knowledgeable look she said -`it's gone that way'. The whole family responded to her directions and when I realised that she had three hundred and sixty degrees of the compass to choose from, I marvel at the fact that she rarely got it wrong - never out by more than two or three degrees. The household could never settle until the insect was caught and capital punishment meted out.

At this, Mother was at her best. One of us would spot the cowering flea and point it out to her. Stealthily she would approach the spot, moistening her thumb and forefinger as she did so on her lips. Then with the speed of a striking king cobra snake her hand streaked out and triumphantly she would hold her thumb and forefinger up to the light making a gentle rolling motion until she could see a small brown leg protruding from her nipped up flesh. At this point she rarely failed and the battle was won. Her other thumb was brought into action as the tiny creature tried to escape but relentlessly it was crushed between her two thumb nails. Next came the inquest - who had we been playing with? - whose house had we been in? etc., etc. Eventually she would form an opinion as to where the insect had come from and how we should try and avoid further visitations.

The trouble with Mother was that when she was on the trail of an intruder, at the first sighting, she would `whoop' with success. I firmly believe that like walls, fleas have ears and as soon as it heard Mother's `whoop' it was off on an escape route just like a fox when it first hears the baying of the hounds. This made the battle take much longer to win - she should have learned to keep quiet whilst on the hunt.

I have never studied the habits of the common flea but it does appear that one of its favourite feeding grounds was round ones midriff. There relaxing in the warmth of the human body it would sink it's sharp little teeth into your flesh. This was more irritating that painful and within seconds the tiny puncture wound would become inflamed and commence to itch. Around the midriff was something that Mother could live with after all if you could refrain from having the occasional scratch the outside world would be blissfully unaware of your problem. But as it has been known to happen, your visitor may have been very hungry and decided to take a bite at your neck on his way down to his favourite feeding ground, then the world was turned upside down. If you had to appear in public, even in mid summer, a scarf would have to be worn. Failing that, you were put under house arrest until the telltale mark had disappeared. Mother was fanatical about fleas. Two occasions come readily to mind concerning her deep horror of ever being accused of harbouring one of the little creatures. One occasion was that from the age of eight onwards, in the height of the summer, we would in company with a dozen or so other children of both sexes, leap out of bed straight onto our bicycles and head off for the glorious sandy beach of Walberswick. There we would tear off our clothes, slip on our bathing trunks and plunge into the flat blue calm sea.

On this particular day, Mother has said that she and Father were coming to spend the day on the beach and would bring the lunch. She knew the area of the beach where we were bound to be and on arriving there on the high tide mark she found a heap of trousers, shirts, socks, liberty bodices, dresses, knickers and shoes in great abundance. At the age of eight we had little or no modesty. Her sharp eyes soon detected my clothes in the vast heap and they were soon removed, given a good shake and folded up neatly before being placed a few feet away from the rest. That evening she was advising me on the wisdom of keeping my clothes apart from others, I found it difficult to understand what I had done wrong. Giving me a wise look she lowered her voice and said -'You see dear, they might have fleas!'

The other occasion was when Father had gone to Dunwich to attend to someone's swarming bees and on his return he was caught in a summer storm. Just as he got to the outskirts of the village, at Mill Farm, the heavens opened. Leaping from his motorcycle he took shelter in the farm buildings by the roadside. After the storm has passed he carried on homeward and by the time he arrived home he realised full well that he was not alone. Whilst sheltering in the farm buildings he had been joined by many little companions who had remained with him on the journey.

The back door was wide open and Mother was working away in the kitchen when Father arrived on the doorstep looking decidedly sheepish. 'Florence', he said, 'I think I have got a flea. ' Mother took one look at him and gave the first order of battle. `Stand still!' (she said afterwards that she could see the fleas leaping around his shoulder as midgets and gnats dance up and down beside a hedgerow). The next order was `Take off your clothes!' which Father duly did obstinately refusing to take off his vest and pants. He had no intention of revealing all to his young family or to any member of the public who may have been watching. `Come in!' was the next order and Father stepped over the pile of clothes he had discarded. Before firmly closing the back door, Mother reached for the yard broom and swept his clothes well beyond a normal flea's leap away. What happened thereafter I do not have on record as I was not privy to the action. I can only imagine that he was first ordered to strip down to what nature intended and no doubt any of the insects on his pants and vest met a violent death between Mother's thumbnails. Then, I suspect, he was subjected to an intimate body search equal to the indignities as is endured by the modern drug smugglers of today. Finally he was given a clean bill of health and allowed to dress again in clean clothes. What happened to his flea-infested clothes on the doorstep I never did know. Probably they were put to the flames and all his travelling companions went with them.

As I said - a flea in our household caused such havoc in those days. How many children today can claim to have seen one or even heard the name. I can only hope that the Great Architect has realised the error of his ways when he introduced fleas into this world and that he has seen to it that the other side of the great divide remains flea-less. I rest happy with the thought that my dear old Mother is not plagued by such hideous little creatures in her new life beyond.

TWILIGHT DREAMS

Pictures can tell us so much - if they could only speak! It has often been said that a picture speaks a thousand words - an estimate which may be an injustice. Anyone gazing at a picture, if he or she has an inventive mind, could easily conjure up a far more ambitious target.

Every household contains pictures which originate from a creative mind - not the sort which are captured on film - but those that were in the mind of the artist as he applied paint on canvas. I possessed such a picture. It was not colourful, rather dark in structure just browns and greens with a splash or two of grey. The scene it depicted was of a woodland, populated by mature beech trees with a fairly level ground carpet all enveloped by a canopy of the trees. Such as it was, it disallowed the artist any imagination of colours but was without doubt a very beautiful and well-executed oil painting. It was signed by a gentleman with the name of C. ROWE - known in the artistic world as a person of middle status - not off the top shelf but most certainly not off the bottom shelf either!

The artist had given his work the title of `A Gypsy Camp'. His imaginative mind had seen a clearing between the beech trees. A small fire in the centre of the clearing had given him a small opportunity to use a splash of colour - the fire had a red tongue of flame. Two adults and their two children sat beside the fire over which a cooking pot hung from metal stakes. On the edge of the clearing stood a barrel-topped caravan and close by was a flat four-wheeled light cart. Two skewbald ponies contentedly grazed upon what greenery they could find growing amongst the carpet of dried leaves on the woodland floor. There was no fear of them straying far from the scene - their front legs were `hobbled' by a length of rope enabling them to take only very short steps.

It was a very contented scene of a family waiting for their supper - probably the main meal of the day - in late Autumn as the daylight faded quickly away, of two ponies enjoying a well earned rest after pulling their vehicles for several miles from their last camping place, of proud and stately beech trees which had stood sentinel there on that area of woodland for several decades.

The artist had indeed conjured up a most beautiful scene and as I sat in the comfort of my armchair, I could sense all that was happening as the daylight turned to dusk. The aroma of the meal cooking in the pot over the fire was most pleasant. Perhaps it was a rabbit stew or even a couple of hedgehogs gently simmering away which would be appeasing the family's hunger very shortly. There would be carrots, onions, turnips and swede to flavour the supper all craftily taken from the adjacent farmland or gathered from the fields as the family travelled to their new camping place.

The mother lifted the lid off the pot with a stick to see how the meal was progressing. She appeared pleased with what she saw because she entered the caravan, emerging with four plates and a ladle. Calling to her family, they all sat cross-legged on the ground as she dished up their supper. The firelight reflected on their faces and as they ate they spoke in low voices - no doubt commenting on their day's experiences or their enjoyment of the meal. They were a happy family - the children sturdy and well fed, lacking nothing other than an introduction to soap and water. They were all shabbily attired no doubt having no desires for fineries. Having consumed their meal the children were sent to their bed in the barrel-topped caravan. It was not a bed as such - rather a shelf at the rear of the van about 4'/2 feet in width where their parents slept. Beneath the shelf heavy curtains were draped. It was behind these curtains where the children slept. There were not pre-bed rituals such as undressing, washing or cleaning teeth - just jackets and footwear would be removed before relaxing in a sound, contented, subconscious state. Outside the ponies would turn head to wind, remain on their feet rock fast but they too would relax into a subconscious state.

The scene has now quiet and settled down signifying that yet another day was almost past. Low conversation was exchanged between the parents before the mother retired into the caravan. Her husband tidied up the fire to make it safe for the night - a little loose earth was placed around the fire which would ensure that the breeze would not fan the flames or spread sparks. This earth would be pulled away in the morning - the fire raked through and a handful of dried leaves would soon create a flame so they could all have morning tea and breakfast when daylight reappeared. Father then entered the caravan and closed the lower half door. All was peaceful and deathly quiet.

Then a Nightjar swept along the edge of the woodland whirring and churring his way low over the ground - his large wide beak agape to collect any insects that got in his way as he glided along. An owl hooted enquiringly from nearby in the woods and was quickly answered by his kinsman way back in the woods.

The pale moon had now appeared through the tall beeches, casting a little light into the woodland. Brer Fox cautiously appeared, scenting the ground as he trotted along searching for the odd rabbit or vole. He would not stay long in the wood where there was little or no scrub to conceal himself - he would be in danger and preferred large open spaces.

Another world was appearing before my eyes - one which I am quite sure the artist was completely unaware of. The long-standing inhabitants of the beech wood were now appearing on stage. Rustling leaves and the occasional snap of a twig indicated that the nocturnal creatures - voles, field mice and rabbits - all were setting out to dine unaware that watchful eyes were noting every movement.

The small brown owls sat in the lower branches communicating with their soft hoots. Their large cousin - the White Owl - glided silently through the trees resting occasionally, his everturning head looking in every direction, his wide-open eyes seeing everything in detail. The small creatures of the wood scurried over and under the leafy carpet as they rummaged for grubs, beech-mast and any other of nature's bounties which lay between the trees. In a flash the peaceful scene erupted into chaos. Terror reigned as the large White Owl swooped to the ground amidst a flurry of leaves and feathers, rising gracefully into the night air bearing a vole in it's talons. Death had struck swiftly. In those few seconds the violent face of nature had been revealed - the hungry would be fed and life would go on again in much the same way as before.

A few minutes later the tranquillity of the night was restored, the rustle of leaves again indicated that the creatures of the wood were foraging again for food. The night would continue to pass by slowly until the first streaks of dawn appeared - sending them scuttling underground to comparative safety before hunger drove them out again the following night to face the hidden dangers and more.

As the night passed the embers of the fire glowed. The owls called to each other from their territory in the wood. Brer Fox could be heard barking in the distant fields. The first sign of dawn appeared and sound came from the caravan. A multitude of rooks approached and settled on the canopy chattering and squabbling noisily. Very soon they would be off to plunder the newly sown fields of winter corn, filling their crops with wheat and barley. As the sun rose and cast it's rays through the trees, the bird life increased. Tree creepers and nut hatches would busily circle each tree prising out any insect which hid in the bark or lurked in any small crevice.

As the sun strengthened children's voices could be heard within the caravan. The adults were now outside, the fire had been cleared of the loose earth, which surrounded it during the night and dead wood had been collected and placed on the fire. Over the fire the kettle was suspended and it steamed merrily away.

The violence of the night had abated and was forgotten. A new day was breaking and innocence prevailed. Life was appearing on all sides, the day would wear on much the same as the day before. Perhaps the gypsy family would move on seeking pastures new and the great beech woodland would await its next visitors, silently and patiently. No sign would remain of the previous occupants - the fire would be raked over, unburnt embers buried in the soil and all rubbish removed.

As I emerged from my comatose condition, I found my picture strangely still and unforgiving, unwilling to reveal its secrets or disclose the nature of the happenings which I had just witnessed. It remained an innocent, tranquil scene of a peaceful woodland to be gazed upon and admired.

ONWARD - TO FURTHER PROGRESS

Harken back to yesterday
When village life began,
Farmsteads all around us
Providing work for man.
Industry sorely needed
Creating wealth and trade,
From farm was born the blacksmith
And farming tools were made.
The village builder in our midst
Providing homes for all,
Shelters for the livestock - jobbing at the Hall.
The humble rabbit catcher
Wheelwright and the thatcher,
Every working hand
Bonded by common purpose
Earned their living off the land.
The ring of the blacksmith's anvil
And the wheelwright's constant blow
Drone of the threshing tackle
The noise of long ago.
But progress has a changing face
And farms fall in decay
Villagers - a forgotten race
Bureaucracy has its say.
But where have we all now got to
Our village quiet and still -
Rejecting all that used to be
Our wealth, our work, our industry?
Our planners look in horror
For if we dare apply
To create again some useful work
To help both man and boy
No noise they say - it's against the plan
And spoils the amenity
Care not for the wants of boy or man
To rebuild the community.
We do not want these changes
All enterprise must cease
Doff your cap as you pass by in silence
May the village rest in peace.

I WILL NEVER FORGET

There are many instances in our lives when certain occurrences bite deep into our memories. These can relate to both happiness and sadness, the latter often goes hand in hand with remorse and feelings of guilt.

The time, which is engraved deep on my memory, was, I believe, in 1936. It happened in the school playground. My childhood was unbelievably happy. I have been so fortunate and been cocooned in security and home comforts with unlimited affection bestowed on me by the best parents any child could ever have. Many children were less fortunate and may have led a completely miserable existence.

Our house was situated on the fringe of the village and was the only one to have a flush toilet and a bathroom. People at that time were very poor but worked hard, existing mainly on the own garden produce, rabbit meat and the cheap fish when it was in season. On a late autumn, early winter after-noon the entire village was enveloped in a delicious aroma of herrings being cooked over an open fire, ready for the breadwinner and his children when he returned from his daily labours.

Every village had its elementary school it was a rare event it any normal child left school without a modicum of general knowledge and a good grasp of the essential three 'R's'. The education authorities in their wisdom had decided that area schools should be constructed and upon reaching the age of 11 years, children should leave village schools and attend an area school.

The year was 1931 and whilst I was only nine years old, my sister was two years older and came into the category of being eligible for area school education. The nearest area school was five miles distance from our village and to make matter worse - the road, which we would have to traverse, was quite busy even in those days it could be dangerous to young children on bicycles. Father was opposed to this and decided that we would attend the elementary school at Wenhaston - half the distance - and for some reason or other, not affected by the new ruling.

At the time there were many orphans in rural areas and some of these unfortunate children were `farmed out' or `housed' in village households. The boarding allowance was the princely sum of ten shillings per week for each child. Some foster homes 'housed' four or five of these orphans and with out doubt inscrutable foster parents accepted the children because it was profitable. Food and love were thin on the ground whilst the ten shillings paid for each child was an income in very difficult days. Children who were not farmed out lived in 'homes', which were specially constructed. Consequently, boys housed there became known as "Home Boys". One such Home was situated at Holton just outside the town of Halesworth - probably four miles from Wenhaston. For some strange reason those children all attended Wenhaston School.

There were no bicycles for them although the Education Authority issued out new cycles to each child that left a village school to attend an area school. These unfortunate children had to walk to school - every day - in any weather and then back to the 'Home' at the end of the school day. I seem to recall that they were sent off with some form of packed lunch - of dubious quality no doubt. They attended school in all weathers - sunshine or rain - poorly clothed, hungry, unloved and unwashed. On wet days they arrived at school drenched to the skin. At the best of times they never smelt clean and when they were wet, the odour was most unpleasant.

I had been at Wenhaston School for a period of probably four years when my moment of truth befell - leaving a deep scar on my memory, which I have never forgotten. The year was probably 1934 or 1935. One of the local village boys had been sent to school with an orange to eat in the morning break from lessons. This was indeed a rare occasion because oranges, at that time, were very much a luxury. I can still picture him, standing in the playground with a group of boys as he peeled his orange, then walked over to a garbage bin into which he dropped the orange peel. I can also still see the 'Home Boy' who followed him. Retrieving the orange peel and eating it ravenously, the look on his face was unforgettable.

I related this incident to my mother who listened in stunned silence, deeply disturbed. Thereafter, when apples were plentiful she would fill my saddle-bag with apples making me promise to ensure that they were given to the 'Home Boys'.

Reflecting back on all this, I realise that this incident took place when World War II was rapidly approaching and within a few years, these unfortunate boys would have been drafted into the services. This would have been their only chance of gaining freedom from oppression, establishing their own dignity and independence and forgetting their only crime - that of being a 'Home Boy'.

OF RICHES UNTOLD

Being born and brought up in a Suffolk village with an elementary schooling, never gave any young person an insight into the world of high finance. This did not mean that we did not enjoy our lives, in fact we lived it to the full. The means of communication were limited - no television or complex, telephone based, high-tech inventions such as the fax or E-Mail were available, to enlighten us with what progressed beyond the village boundaries.

Months came and went with little change compared with earlier years. Woodlands came into colour each Spring and their canopies gave shelter to a multitude of small birds. Animal life was limited - the local estates usually kept a herd of deer which did not roam beyond the park which stretched out in front of the Big Hall.

The occasional sighting of a fox, badger or otter gave us quite a lot to talk about for a week or so. In the main very little excitement came into our lives. In the area where I was born - Blythburgh, Wenhaston, Bramfield - all agricultural areas - good hearty farming land produced some farmers who without doubt accumulated a `bit of money' over the years. Inevitably, several dealers were attracted to the area - dealing in cattle, livestock of all types, property and cars.

Cars were, at the time, very thin on the road. The A12 turnpike, as it was known, would be empty for half an hour or more before a single car appeared. After nightfall it would be quite rare to get a sighting of any vehicle. The farmers and dealers nearly all had a vehicle - only a few years before their means of transport had been a pony and trap. A car denoted some level of opulence and any car owner could not hide the fact that he had a penny or two stowed away somewhere.

Perhaps it was this which attracted a gentleman into our midst who oozed opulence. His well presented appearance - neat dark suit, bowler hat and the accompanying rolled up umbrella - spoke volumes. His history was unknown except for the fact that he had a distinct military bearing and claimed the rank of Major. Obviously a very clever man, he booked into the Swan Hotel at Southwold from where he planned his business operations.

Major Crane left no stone unturned. He made it his duty to find out who were the `moneyed' people in the area. He sought them out in all the villages - usually by visiting the local public houses. Word soon spread and he became a household name. Everyone knew of him, many went out of their way to meet him, and with little exception, they were all impressed.

He was a breath of fresh air in the normal dull village life - for he came to bear good news. He had the sole rights to a gold mine in South Africa and intended to enhance its already lucrative production by selling shares. The locals were very lucky indeed that by just passing through, he had noted certain things, which had interested him and it was out of good fortune that he had decided to stay for a few day and get to know the area and the people. We simple villagers were about to be initiated into the world of high finance.

The year was, I believe, 1935 or 36. The major was a shrewd operator. He would make friends with the wealthiest farmer in each village, throw an evening party at the farmhouse and ask the farmer to invite all his friends and neighbours. He entertained them lavishly and as they mellowed over a glass of scotch, they all fired questions to him about his gold mine.

No doubt he was a good talker and when he had decided that the net was full of fish he played his trump card. At his own expense, he would take them all to London where the plans could be seen, his solicitor and accountant would be on hand ready to explain the benefits of this golden opportunity and answer their queries. This was arranged and, at the appointed hour, a large Charabanc arrived in the village and some thirty to forty local farmers and dealers, all in their Sunday best attire, would head off to London. Probably none of them had even been to the Metropolis before and it was indeed a very exciting and impressive day out.

Where they went to in London was never known. However, in the heart of the city, the Charabanc stopped outside a large town house. Major Crane got off the bus and rang the doorbell of the impressive building. The door was opened by a manservant who bowed and scraped as was the custom in those days. The entire entourage filed into the impressive drawing room where on a large polished table, the drawings and documents of the Major's gold mine were laid out for display. Two city gents, dressed impeccably, stood by to explain and answer any questions.

A butler with a silver salver brought around the drinks and those old Suffolk lads, they were indeed, in Aladdin's Cave. It was never revealed how many of these fortune seekers took out their cheque-books and purchased shares. They were told that their share certificates would take a little time to process but should land on their doorsteps in a week or so.

The elated gentlemen were returned safely to the village and for days the villagers were alive with the stories of what these lucky investors had seen in London. Perhaps some who had not taken up the Major's offer lost sleep at night and cursed themselves at their stupidity at not joining in.

Of course the Major did not return to Southwold - his task was completed. Day after day passed by and no share certificates were delivered. The cheques had all been cashed in a London bank and as time lengthened the penny dropped. No one had thought of getting the Major's address, being driven around the Metropolis had confused them all and to look for the impressive house where they had parted with their cheques was like looking for a needle in a haystack.

Eventually the police were informed and they began their task of finding the elusive 'Major'. The daily papers and the Sunday issues all got wind of it. Reporters descended on our sleepy village and the headlines in all papers read *The Wenhaston Millions, '.* Local rags delighted the men who gathered around the bar in the local pub with jokes which circulated about Major Crane and the Wenhaston Millions! It had indeed, through the media such as existed then, become a national topic.

It was many weeks before the Major felt the hand of the law on his shoulder and no doubt by then, he had found another locality where some rich pickings could be gathered. But the Bow Street Runners did eventually catch up with him and his trial in London resurrected the excitement and the gossip and speculation enriched the buzz of conversation around every bar.

So many years have now passed and my memory has dimmed considerably. I do recall that the 'Major' found himself a guest of His Majesty's and languished in prison for a few years. In those days crime was almost unheard of. What of today? Would such an incident now have such reverberations as did the 'Major's' incursion into Suffolk? This I would very much doubt. Our enlightened judiciary would most likely slap his wrist and award him a hundred hours community service!

ATTENDING SCHOOL IN THE 1927-1937 ERA

We live in a changing world as did our forefathers but without doubt the changes take place much more rapidly now and are more far reaching today than ever before.

School age began, in my young days, when you reached your fifth birthday and ended when you had attained the age of fourteen or fifteen. On your first day at school, your Mother would accompany you to the playground where some elder child, known to you, would take charge to begin what was, in your young and tender years, a most formidable experience. If you lived any distance from the school, your Mother would have packed up your lunch, together with a bottle of lemonade, cold tea or cocoa. Memory has a habit of failing after many years, or at least it does in detail, and becomes difficult to bring into focus, yet after sixty years, as I write, my mind is already at work. Some time in August 1927, my Mother delivered me to the school and ultimately into the safe keeping of Miss Stella Dean - Headmistress of Blythburgh Elementary School. No doubt it would have been most difficult to assess who shed the most tears - Mother or I! Blythburgh School consisted, I seem to remember, of two large classrooms - one which was divided by a sliding or folding partition. The rooms were heated by large open coal fires and, as it was in those days, most of the heat went up the chimney and was ineffective. The fortunate children whose desks were placed in the front of the class, did manage to feel warm as did the teacher - whose desk was placed most conveniently to get this benefit. Those children at the rear of the class were far less fortunate and were quite cold for most of the time. Miss Stella Dean was ably assisted by another teacher - Miss Vivien Green, a young lady not many years out of college. The fact that an elder brother of mine courted her brought me no favours that I can recollect. Miss Green was, I believe, of local origin whereas Miss Dean was forever telling all and sundry that her birthplace was 'Ull-on-the-'Umber, a fact that she related with great pride.

In your early days at school you were placed in the infants class, which was not too stringent in its administration. From there you would progress into `Standard I' and each year "examinations" took place and upon your academical merit you moved up through Standards II, III, and IIII. From Standard IIII, it was normal to leave school and commence work. Girls would usually go into "Service" - another way of describing domestic duties. They would become maids in the larger and more wealthy family homes - usually `living in'. Boys were more fortunate and had far more choice. Many would go to work with their fathers on the local farms. Some, whose parents had more foresight, were enrolled into apprenticeship with the local tradesmen, learning the trade of the local wheelwright, blacksmith or builder. Others would get work delivering groceries or meat on a trade bicycle to all the village and the outlaying district.

Perhaps the best opportunity was to become a Telegram Boy for the Post Office. Telegrams were then a popular way of communication and boys would be issued with a bright red bicycle and telegrams, messages in a sealed envelope, would be delivered by them over a wide area. Pay was small then whatever work you had but the Post Office offered the best opportunity for promotion to any enterprising young lad who was not afraid of work. However, schools then were not the comfortable establishments such as they are today. The playground was an area surrounding the school - of just plain earth - no concrete or tarmacadam. It was muddy in winter and dusty in summer. Attached to the school was a lean-to entrance porch. This was quite large and the walls were furnished with rows of hooks upon which outer garments were hung whilst the owners were in the classroom. There were always two or three large galvanised buckets filled with an enamel drinking mug ready for any child wishing to quench its thirst. There was also one or two hand basins in the porch together with a clean towel and a large black or red, strong carbolic soap to allow the washing of hands, etc.

In those long gone days village folks were, in the main, quite poor. Every village had it's local `Squire' or person who was far better off than most of the villagers. Therefore toys and material objects of leisure were not available to most people. Children had to devise their own pleasures and pastimes as best they could. Each spring, as the days lengthened, children would amuse themselves with hoops. A hoop was a metal ring of about three feet in diameter made quite cheaply by the local blacksmith, or the rim of a cycle wheel would serve the same purpose, persuaded to bowl along the road with the aid of a short stick. This kept children running around for hours. The summer heralded the arrival of the marble season. These little round balls of clay, baked hard and painted in bright colours, were found in every child's pocket. There would be contests in the playground where a small hole, the size of a bird's nest, was scraped out of the bare earth. A line was drawn in the soil about ten feet away where the players would stand and toss the marbles towards the hole. Each player would then take turns in trying to flick the marbles into the hole with the crook of their index finger. Once in the hole the marbles were won by the person who had flicked them into the hole. Summer also brought football and cricket for the boys usually played on a farmer's meadow where the cows grazed. For goal posts just two jackets would be placed on the grass. Both boys and girls would collect wild berries for their Mother to make jam or sell to the shops to earn a few pence pocket money. Autumn evenings saw the appearance of spinning tops. These would be lashed up and down the road with the aid of a small homemade whip. They would spin through the air for quite long distances. There was very little danger on the roads then - perhaps only a dozen cars would drive through the village in a day. Autumn also brought in the conker season. Ripe horse chestnuts were gathered, threaded onto a length of string and players would take turns in shattering the opponents conker which was held out for the attack by other players who struck at it with a downward swipe. Other pastimes were fishing for roach in the local ponds, birds nesting, recording car numbers and many other activities. Back in school, lessons were rigidly conducted with discipline and respect. Children would arrive in the playground and run around or chatter as they pleased. At 9 am prompt, a teacher would ring a brass hand bell. From that moment all chattering ceased. Not a word was allowed to be spoken. The children fell into single file and made their way sedately to their classroom and took their seat at their desk. The teacher would then call out each child's name from the school register. As their name was called the child would answer *"Present, Miss"* and a tick would be put against their name. If a child was absent with no note of explanation from their parents, this would be reported to the school attendance officer who would call on the parents to find out why the child was not at school.

After the register has been called, lessons would begin in earnest. Children were expected to be attentive at all times, remain seated and remain silent. They would have to ask the teacher if they could be excused should they wish to visit the toilet or for any other reason. The toilets then were quite primitive - just a row of brick built cubicles sited at the back of the playground to the rear of the school. There was no running water, each cubicle was equipped with a large galvanised bucket which would be emptied by one of the men from the village at the end of each day. Should any child fail to behave or break any of the school rules, he or she would receive strokes of the cane across their outstretched palm. This stinging punishment was most effective and miscreants did not readily commit the same offence again in a hurry. Miss Stella Dean was, in my opinion, always too eager to administer this corporal punishment and when an offence had been committed or damage occurred and no-one was prepared to admit being the culprit, she would order the whole class to stand in line and hold their hands out before she proceeded along the line dealing a hefty swipe at each hand that was held out. On one occasion, mine being one of them. However, apart from that, I greatly respect and value the education I received at Blythburgh School. It was a simple and well disciplined education which has never brought me any honours or distinctions - yet! I was left able to read, write and count as life required. It taught me to show respect and kindness to others at all times. It taught me to stand up for myself and to appreciate opportunities as they came along and when one did appear - to grab it by the forelock for the back of it's head was bald!

THE OLD WASP CHEWER

Having suffered the misfortunes and frustrations of living in close proximity to a female neighbour who kept me under close surveillance, regularly reporting me anonymously for breaching regulations to local Council Authorities, Forestry Commission etc, etc she was known as `the old wasp chewer' because of her peculiar habit of chewing her gums and permanent scowl she had due to those facial manoeuvres. I penned these short lines:

> I cannot stand up and be counted
> I dare not disclose my name
> What kind of person am I?
> To achieve this level of fame?

OBEDIENCE

A well-known East Anglian publican, way back in the mid 1960s, kept a liver and white Springer Spaniel, which was named Paddy. Each evening, nearing closing time, the landlord would open the bar door and let Paddy out for his last exercise of the day. Allowing the dog ten minutes or so, the landlord would go to the back door and blow his whistle, known as a `silent dog whistle'. Within a minute Paddy would come scuttling back around the corner and into the bar. A lady, who had witnessed this occurrence many times, could not control her admiration of understanding between man and dog any longer.

"Wonderful. What obedience! How on earth did you train him to obey your command so readily?"

To which our landlord replied, "Well, ma-am, it's bike this - when I blow, he know, he's gotta come, Dew he don't - he git my foot up his backside!"

--ooOoo--

GOOD ADVICE

A Suffolk couple, having suffered each other for forty years of turbulent marriage, were continuing their daily battle of words. George, who was reclining on the couch, was reading the daily newspaper. Hilda was trying to tidy up and hoover the carpet and reminded him every five minutes that the garden hedge needed clipping, the lawn needed mowing and if he did not get off his backside and get some sausages from the butchers, he would get no lunch. George rewarded her continuous barracking with stony silence.

Exasperated, she said, "If I ever come back in the world I hope that I will return as a man!" Quietly George replied, "A word of advice for you if your wish is granted. Having experienced life in this world as a man - just don't get married!

NO GOOD WILL COME OF IT ON A SUNDAY!

Thus spoke Florence Elizabeth Clarke many times during my childhood days. Mother was born in 1901 close to the `Eels Foot Inn' at Theberton. One of a family of five, she endured a very hard and difficult life. He father, the breadwinner, was a rabbit warrener and very skilful at his trade. The family never went hungry but existed very well on a diet of rabbit meat plus the occasional pheasant which was unfortunate enough to get caught in one of grandfather's snares.

I know very little of the family's religious followings only from what I can remember of the conversations I enjoyed with her in later years. However, it would appear that the family were chapel-goers and unless I have misunderstood, like many other chapel people of that era, grandfather would at times act as a lay-preacher. When Mother was about four years old the family moved from Theberton and took up residence in one of the two cottages which stand on the Blythburgh Fen. The other cottage was occupied by Charlie Muttit, one of the gamekeepers employed on the expansive Blois Estate when it included the Fen area. Charlie's son, Percy Muttit, who also devoted his life to gamekeeping for the estate, lives in the same cottage to this very day. From the Fen every day, Mother and her brothers and sisters would walk to Blythburgh to attend the Village School, a distance of between three and four miles. Nothing would prevent this ritual other than a heavy snowfall after which the Fen would be completely cut off from the outside world until kinder times arrived and a thaw set in. Therefore, on damp, wet days the children would arrive at school very wet and cold, many of her classmates would be in a similar uncomfortable state but had the added burden of being quite hungry as well. The main classroom at the school has a large open fireplace and there was never a shortage of coal and the teachers would do their best to dry what outer garments they could. If the rain persisted all day the children would tramp all the way home getting cold and wet once again. This time it was their Mother's turn to try and get their clothes dry during the evening in order to send them off back to school the next morning. But in the meantime, the family would be warmed up with good hot food and by the roaring log fire which kept the cottage warm. No doubt evenings were kept short and the children were packed off to bed quite early so as not to be late in the morning. Bedtime was made as comfortable as possible by the placing of house bricks in the open fire for an hour before they were taken out, wrapped well in strips of old blankets and placed in the beds ready to receive the cold feet of the occupants as they retired for the night.

Saturdays were non-school days but it was not a day for children to waste their time. All of them had to take a share of the family chores and according to the season, they would have to collect dead branches and sticks ready to be chopped up as `kindling' to get enough heat into the fire for it to accept logs or coal. Spring and Summer months would be spent on collecting the wild berries and fruit, which would be preserved and stacked away in the larder for next winter.

After arriving home, the children would take it in turns to fetch the milk from the nearby farm. This was carried in enamelled cans, complete with lid, capable of carrying two pints. But Sundays were kept as days of rest and any idea of being industrious or creative on that day were rapidly knocked on the head with the stern rebuke "No good will come of it on a Sunday". Quite a narrow-minded vision really when one considers that somebody had to work on Sunday to feed all the animals. Somebody has to bring in the herd of cows and milk them before putting them back out to grass. Trains were speeding across the country carrying mail, which would be anticipated and delivered the following morning. Policemen would be required to patrol their beat and uphold the law.

So just how the good country folk came to accept this belief and administer such stern cautions to any would-be breaker of the Sunday truce is quite hard to understand. But such was the disciples that Mother received and in due course instilled this into her own children. Every Sunday the whole family would put on their best attire, the children would be well scrubbed and preened and they would tramp the four miles in Blythburgh where they would attend all three services held there in the Wesleyan Chapel. Sandwiches and cake would enable them to survive the day and after the evening service was concluded the family were rounded up and the long tramp home began early to bed ready to face the next day's trials and tribulations.

So it is easy to understand how Mother's stern warning came to be imprinted well on my mind. Even the loss of her brother who fell in the Battle of the Somme at eighteen years of age - a loss which she never overcame in her 82 years - failed to shake her belief in keeping Sunday hallowed. She probably never thought that even wars were a seven days a week affair. I must have been born with rebel instincts because as I approached my `teens, she capitulated and I was able to spend the whole weekend on a nearby farm where we roamed freely with air-guns, catapults, ferreted the hedgerows and caught rabbits and the occasional long-tail. In fact I did all that went against Mother's old adage of "No good will come of it on a Sunday". But until then I remained well within the fold. At Mother's insistence, we appeared every Sunday dressed in our best attire and relaxed on the day of rest. Father went along with this and he did little else than read the Sunday newspapers, complete the News of the World crossword and help Mother complete the fashion competition in the `People'. Probably by then Mother had forsaken her chapel attendance because of Father's attitude on the subject of religion. He professed to be a non-believer but some time - well back in my memories of the early days - I distinctly remember as a family attending the Holy Trinity Church at Blythburgh where as he entered the pew and sat down, he adopted the pose of the firm believer and went through the correct rituals. The occasion must have been a wedding - possibly a funeral and was indeed a one-off event.

However, my sister and I were never instructed to go to church or Sunday School. We did attend Sunday School at times but did so voluntarily - it was never mandatory. We did our own thing. Mother never cooked on Sunday to the best of my recollection. We lived off cold meat and mashed potatoes. Mother did violate Sunday truce in a small way because she was never idle. She would have a pile of socks beside her, which she darned quickly and neatly. Any patch which was not darned neatly was, in her eyes, -`cobbled'. She would wear her best frock - one which she had previously sat down and made with her own fair hands - every stitch neat and precise. She never referred to that garment as being a dress and when attired that way she was at leisure. Other days it was a skirt and blouse - sleeves rolled up and she was at work. On Sunday the linen line in the back garden behind the house remained bare. Not a single handkerchief would be allowed to flutter in the breeze. Yet within hours, on the following morning, it would be full of snow-white or perhaps Reckitt blue. Linen blowing in the wind like sails at sea - a rare sight and a pleasure to behold - now a practice long since gone the work being taken over by an electric tumble dryer.

Sundays just had to be kept as a day of rest and like many other country families we often indulged in the afternoon walk. This usually embraced a leisurely stroll covering some four or five miles. Father always had his walking stick and his black boots were well polished to perfection. On these walks we often met other families also out on their Sunday walk. We would stop a few minutes and much small talk was indulged in before we proceeded on our way. The route taken would be Father's choice and he liked to leave the hard road and walk across fields by way of farm tracks, bridle paths and sometimes just following hedgerows. It was on one of these walks that I well remember meeting Charlie Muttit, the gamekeeper. Whilst we were keeping to the paths and not damaging crops, it was of course possible that we disturbed the odd pheasant especially in nesting time, but we did not really break any rules. However, Charlie resented anyone trespassing on his patch however well behave they might be and although he knew Mother and Father very well, he was obliged to make it quite clear that he disapproved.

In his slow Suffolk dialect he eyed Father up and down and said "My word, how yew tigether dew go about!" Of course he could have added to that by saying "No good will come of it on a Sunday!"

Ready to face the world. Arthur, Tony Fiske, Arthur Sharman, Joe Hurren and two unknown boys.

MY FIRST JOB

Wenhaston Elementary School was my seat of learning. I readily admit that I was never a good scholar and would suggest that had a list of placings on merit been available, my name would have appeared will down in the lower half. Modesty prevents me from suggesting otherwise.

Our Headmaster, Louis J Sangster by name, was better known to his pupils as Lu-Lu. He was a dapper little fellow always dressed immaculately, his suit was pressed each day, and a clean white handkerchief neatly tucked into the cuff of his shirtsleeve. Never would it be seen in his pocket - he believed it would in some way make his suit appear to be misshapen! On reaching the age of thirteen, I had little or no desire to sit at a school desk. I felt that the world was waiting for me. Being a strong, healthy and well-fed lad I thought I was well able and quite capable of taking my place in the world of responsibility. Whilst I was never a troublesome lad, I always thrived on a good sense of humour - a quality which Lu-Lu was almost entirely deficient of. Therefore, it was inevitable that at times he and I clashed head on and in his highly regarded position of Headmaster of the village school he had to struggle hard to maintain his image and dignity when dealing with growing lads of my stature. Then the year being 1937, there were no holds barred. Lu-Lu had a selection of canes in his desk but rather wisely decided not to attempt to administer corporal punishment in my direction. Instead he would grasp my shoulders and attempt to shake me into submission. I learned to stand rock-fast and Lu-Lu would shake like mad - his energy unable to transfer to my rock like stance, it was always he whose head nearly came off his shoulders in the attempt.

It was then that I decided it was only fair to him that I should leave school. I had no parental persuasion to do so and I had no job to go to. Neither had I any inclination of what I wanted to do with my life. At that time, living in a Suffolk village in a predominantly agricultural area, lads leaving school had little choice of work. Working on the farm, apprentice to the local blacksmith, wheelwright, delivering meat or groceries for the local shop on a trade bicycle or becoming a Telegram Boy at the Post Office - there was little else on offer. The best opportunity was to become a Telegram Boy - there was a sequence of promotions where a bright and willing lad could eventually become a postman or even a Post Master.

I decided that none of these avenues were really for me and whilst I now readily admit that I really had little or no ambition, I was drifting. Being a very capable young poacher, I kept my mother well supplied in game and always sold enough rabbits and game to provide me with pocket money. My eldest brother whom I was always very close to, was at that time working at the Empire Pool, Wembley part of the stadium complex. I asked him if he could find me a job and it so transpired that an opportunity came up for me to work in the electricians department at the Empire Pool.

Mother packed my case and I got on the old steam train at Halesworth en route for Liverpool Street where brother George met me. I soon found myself at Wembley and in the safe custody of Mr and Mrs Hinton at 56 Linden Avenue where I was to lodge during my employment at the Empire Pool. I cannot recall the month I started work. The annual programme of events at the Empire Pool included ice skating, swimming, the International Six Day Cycle Race plus other one-off attractions. At that time, the Empire Pool was the largest cantilever type building in Europe. The season commenced with the swimming and diving championships after which the pool was emptied then within the pool, scaffolding was erected and boarded over. Next a smooth wooden cycle track was constructed with elevated bends at the ends of the oval circuit. The bends had a very steep camber whilst the long sides had much less. It was an international event. Each nation had a team of two riders - one of whom had to be on the circuit for the 24 hours throughout the whole six days.

After that the cycle track was taken up and refrigeration tubes were laid on the boards which cover the pool. Sand was spread just to cover the tubes then sprayed with water. The refrigeration was then switched on and the sand froze. Constant spraying enabled a two-inch layer of ice to form and the large oval ice rink was ready to house the events. I worked with the electricians between the events putting in new contact points and sockets, placing microphones at the required places and testing the equipment, etc. Again I cannot recall just how long I was employed but I know that I did see the full programme of events right through - it must have been at least a year. I learned to skate using ice hockey tubes, which were much faster than figure skates - I pride myself that I was a `natural'.

Wembley had two ice hockey teams - Wembley Lions and Wembley Tigers. There was also a band of young lads training to play ice hockey. They were known as the Wembley Cubs. I often skated with them as the practised between the sessions when the public was using the rink.

It was during one of these sessions for the public that I got to know 'Sabu' - the elephant boy. He was a regular visitor and I often skated with him. I also got to know most of the stars of the ice hockey world - Lew Bates, the Lemay Brothers, Frankie Cadorey and many others. I also met Hans Gerchweiller - the reigning men's figure skating champion and his brother Arnold who was his trainer/ manager. When the events were taking place and the electricians had little to do, only maintenance, I was given the job of playing piped music whilst the band were at rest or off duty. I had my own little room, which was known as the `Gramophone Room'. This was fitted with a twin pamphonic turntable and racks of records - such as Canadian Leapers, Bugle Call Rag, etc., etc. Not all of them appealed to me but my duty was to play a mixed selection of music, recording each record played in order that `royalties' could be assessed. Perhaps I was the first disc jockey! The ladies figure skating champion then was Cecilia College. She had a record made to her own tempo - it was the Skater's Waltz. She would appear in my little den every time she practised and ask me to play her record. This I would do and she practised her routine. She would return and collect her precious record and she would always give me five shillings. Considering that my wages were a princely sum of 25 shillings of which I paid Mrs Hinton five shillings for my lodgings, this extra five shillings was a godsend. On Thursday nights I had to work over at the stadium where I was placed high in the roof and followed the speedway riders round the circuit with my spotlight. It was there that I met Bluey Wilkinson, an 'Aussie' rider.

Tuesday nights saw me back in the stadium, this time in the Stewards Box where I controlled the electric hare - just keeping it ahead of the greyhounds. I cannot remember ever getting any overtime pay, it was part of the job. However, I was always short of money - a situation which worried me. At that time I was into `wireless' sets and actually built a one valve set from a kit of parts I bought. My pecuniary state plus a distinct homesick feeling, missing all my friends of both sexes back in Suffolk, made me a bit unhappy. I requested an interview with Alan Parsons, head of my department and asked for a rise in pay. It was not forthcoming so the scene was set for me to return home.

I almost forgot to say that on my day off I would leave Wembley early in the morning and made my way to the West End of London just aimlessly walking round. In the evening I would be at the `Old Met' in the Edgeware Road. There I have seen George Robey, Ernie Lottinga, Billy Bennett and most of the old music hall entertainers. Often I would miss the last bus home to Wembley and could only get as far as Stonebridge Park, from there I had to walk the last 4-5 miles.

That concludes a brief history of my first job. So it was back to Mother and a period of poaching before I donned a blue and white striped jacket and peaked cap to start my second job as a Walls ice cream salesman, pedalling a `Stop Me & Buy One' Walls ice cream tricycle - but that's another story!!

PERPETUATION

From the tree
They now dance free
Twirling, swirling - ever dancing
Breeze assisted, sliding - prancing.
Repeating every move anew
Discarded leaves of every hue,
Red and gold, some russet brown
From the tree, they flutter down.
Acrobats - they make no sound
Wind dried, their freedom found,
Free to dance in the autumn sun
Scuttling along, they slide and run
Until at last they dance no longer
Gone in the breeze as the wind grows stronger.
Trapped in a corner - soaked by the rain
They lay and rot - yet to live again
Next Spring, in Nature's perpetual spree
They will appear again, upon the tree.

JEANS

Dirty, scruffy, shapeless bags
Holes in knees and crotch that sags.
Worn by all - from birth to grave
Is there such little face to save?

Who penned those lines, once which said
The dress doth maketh men?
How things have changed - since fashion led
Us on this downward trend.

Call them jeans or denim blue
They are but the dungarees I knew
Thro' the years of my life's span
And were once the dress of the working man.

Boiler suit or bib `n' brace
Jacket and trousers too,
Once denoted a noble race
Of workmen - good and true.

But even then, they would appear
Cleanly washed with darn or patch
No bare flesh beneath the tear
Respect prevailed with dignity to match.

Now this garment, born anew,
Plagues us all, these shades of blue
Bleached in part to catch the eye,
Frayed at bottoms, their shape awry.

There's no escape from this unsightly trend
They are seen in every place.
Confined not to creed or race,
For sex nor age offend.

In planes, on ships, in schools and bar
Church and office - near and far
Across the world - no boundaries
For what are really, dungarees!

THE OLD GYPSY LADY

Blythburgh Lodge, named in most of the old reference books as Westwood Lodge, is sited between Blythburgh and Walberswick. It can be reached by the back road from Walberswick which leads from a fork junction just before reaching the church as you leave the village. There it stands at the end of a hard metalled road which rather abruptly ends and diverges into a gravel and sandy path which winds it's way over the heath, skirting the northern boundary of the Minsmere Nature Reserve, past the Pine Woods and through Blythburgh Fen before it emerges at the Five Cross Ways at Hinton. Alternatively it can be reached by the road leading direct from Blythburgh to Walberswick by turning off the road approximately a mile from the cross-roads, taking an unmade road to the right through the fields. There is a gate across the unmade road and going through this gate, the road leads through what used to be referred to as the Park. It is a large acreage of grassland which was, in the late 1930's, populated by well-grown thorn trees. This area was used to graze the animals and a gate the other side of the Park ensured their security. Leaving the second gate, the unmade road led though the farmyard and past Blythburgh Lodge joining up at the end of the hard metalled road, which is the back road from Walberswick. It is this unmade road, which leads through the Park that this story is centred upon.

Blythburgh Lodge is very old, possibly some 400 years, and during its existence has been a local point for much of the local folklore and stories of strange happenings. It is said that in a part of the Lodge, an accordion can be heard playing in a large cupboard or locker room. A headless horseman has been seen galloping along the back road and into the farm area of the Lodge. An old gamekeeper, long since departed, was quite emphatic that he had witnessed this phenomenon more than once. Many such stories are embraced by this very large and rambling old building and when backed by an old 80-year-old gamekeeper, who could possibly doubt their authenticity?

As a lad, from the age 13 to 16 I was quite familiar with Blythburgh Lodge. My friends were the children of the Farm Manager who was employed at the time by the late Sir Ralph Blois and who lived in the Lodge. Thus it came to pass that I spent many happy hours there and have on one occasion stayed the night there. I well remember laying in bed in the huge old bedroom keeping awake and listening to the soughing of the wind in the old fir trees outside the house. It was at the time of the year when the travelling circus moved around the country and Bertram Mills Circus was booked to perform at the Crown Meadow in Great Yarmouth. On this occasion the Farm Manager has promised to take his wife, two sons and his daughter to see the show. They duly set off for Yarmouth and were soon seated in the Big Top enthralled by the antics of the clowns in the sawdust ring and the performing horses and riders. The big cats were allowed into the ring through the metal barred tunnel and the inevitable elephants did their party piece. Flying high in the Big Top were the trapeze artistes, all very breathtaking to the ordinary country lads and lasses, many of whom had never seen such a performance before. At the end of the show, filing out of the Big Top, the family made their way to their Armstrong Siddely car and were soon on the A12 heading towards Blythburgh. Turning off at Blythburgh White Hart, up to the cross-roads, they took the Walberswick road shortly leaving it to take the unmade road across the fields and through the Park to the Lodge and to their beds which they were looking forward to after having such a grand evening out. It was then getting late - about 11.30 pm.

The eldest son sat in the front of the car with his dad - his mother, brother and sister in the back. Reaching the first gate the farm manager stopped the car, his son got out, opened the gate and closed it again when the car moved through. The headlights of the car picked out the cattle as they grazed in the Park. Getting back in the car beside his dad, the son settled in his seat as the car moved forward across the Park. Without any warning his dad suddenly stamped on his brakes causing his family to be thrown forward from their seats. His wife, quite agitated said to her husband, "What on earth are you doing? Whatever is wrong?"

He replied with a tone of annoyance saying, "That old gypsy woman walked straight in front of the car."

Craning their necks to see, the family all said, "What old woman? Where is she?"

"There!" he replied "Her with the basket and the black shawl!" pointing to the front of the car. It was several minutes before the family proceeded and a very nervous son who got out to open and shut the second gate. Whilst his family saw nothing but the cattle in the Park, to his dying day the Farm Manager was convinced of his sighting of the Old Gypsy Woman. This story was related to me by his wife the next day and eagerly confirmed by his children. The year was probably 1936.

THE FIRST TIME I EVER SAW ONE!

It was well on towards the end of the war when I first saw one.
At the time I was on a ship named Empire Ness and we lay in King
George V Dock in London loading supplies to take to our Armed
Forces as they pushed their way through to Germany and ultimate
victory.

Whilst lying at anchor or on moorings, all ships were safe -
guarded at night by the appointment of one of the crew to be Night
Watchman. This meant that one had to walk round the ship several
times in the hours of darkness to check that mooring ropes were in
order and that the ship was not dragging it's anchor. It was also the
Night Watchman's duty to see all the crew back aboard safely after
an evening out.

Whilst at the dockside, a companion way (set of stairs) was tied
into position to allow men to negotiate their way safely on and off
the ship. The crew would return late in the evening and `turn in'
(the nautical term for going to bed). From that time the ship fell
silent and the Night Watchman would enjoy his supper and remain
vigilant until daylight broke. However, King George V Dock being
on the side of the Thames in the East End of London, there was
never any peace. Searchlights pierced the night sky as the bombers
droned overhead. Red reflections in the sky pinpointed fires all
around the City and the constant bomb explosions shattered the
night air.

This particular evening it was my turn as Night Watchman. I have
regretted many times since then that I have not kept a diary to refer
to for dates of the experiences that befell me almost daily.

However, I was leaning against the ship's rail looking down river
at the night sky when I sensed a low flying plane approaching. As
it appeared in view I noted that it had a light or glow at the rear of
the fuselage. The anti-aircraft guns from Southend to the city had
all fired at this aircraft as it headed towards the densely populated
area of the East End.

I saw it pass through three Box Barrages (multi barrelled guns
firing salvos of 20-30 shells in one burst) but the plane never
deviated. It carried on a straight course up river. I knew then that I
had seen a plane with no pilot on board - no human could have
flown through that barrage without deviating course.

I called the crew at 7.00 am and fetched their breakfast from the galley. Telling them of what I had seen in the early hours, they all laughed at my statement, suggesting I had dropped off to sleep and dreamt of this - or that I had been drinking too much! At 10.00 am the next morning the whole dock was a hive of activity. Cranes were swinging from dock to ship with huge cargo nets all over the docks. A transit shed to our left was feeding hundreds of troops through to a troop carrying vessel moored close by. Then it happened - one of the pilot-less planes I had seen earlier approached. It's engine cut out and it dived into the dock within a 100 feet of our ship. Then another was followed in quick succession by many more. One fell on the transit shed killing scores of the embarking soldiers. Pandemonium broke out as these planes rained down on the London Dock area. I had witnessed the first Doodle-Bug that crashed on London - it was the first time I had ever seen one but most certainly was not the last!

THE ENCOUNTER

No words were said -
But her mind I read.
In those fleeting seconds of time
When her eyes met mine.

Beauty - supreme in elegance
Held me - helpless in a trance.
Mutual too was the feeling
Our hearts on fire - senses reeling.

The message came, precise and clear.
With perfect ease - no thought of shame
She would share my life - my bed - my name
Her honest face portrayed no fear.

How great then - is Nature's force
Which diverts strangers from their course
Completely from their normal run
And moulds two people into one?

Yet it's fate who has the final say
For to claim my prize I could not stay
The call to board at Gate Forty Nine
Told me then - she would not be mine!

Just one last glance as I made my way
Her appealing eyes were calling me.
But duty first, I had to flee
Whilst she stood still for she must stay.

While cruising high at the speed of sound,
I dreamed of this love -just newly found.
Such beauty, radiant and supreme,
And the partnership which might have been.

My thoughts and dreams of her alone
I could not share with anyone.
Above the clouds - high in the skies
Of azure blue - as were her eyes.

They said it all, they spoke the most
Of a conquest which I cannot boast.
Had a roll of the dice or a turn of fate,
Deprived me of the perfect mate?

MATHEMATICS

Though many years have passed with me
I well recall that seven nines are sixty-three.
No aid require to keep my brain alive
Reminding me that five thirteen's are sixty-five!

This knowledge has remained in store
Since I learned my tables from the age of four
No illusions - no magic tricks
To know that eight times seven is fifty-six.

No electronic gadget required by me
To add together twenty-one and forty two.
A simple sum which all should know
Amounts to a total of sixty three.

When in a shop it's common sense
To think of pound as a hundred pence.
So what I bought for eighty three
Means seventeen in change for me.

So why - when I ask for six costing nine
Does the young lady ring her box of tricks.
Six times - just to find
That she need fifty-four and I need forty-six?

I WRITE MY OWN EPITAPH

It was late in July 1922 when I first entered the `Theatre of Life'. As the years elevated me to maturity I came to realise what a wonderful and beautiful spectacular I was being privileged to watch.
The exquisite stage setting and props, all supplied by Mother Nature, are quite beyond understanding and defy description. The great range of colours with it's many scents, arising from small seeds barely visible to the eye. The many tons of oak timber produced from a single acorn, the minute insects and the creatures large and small.
The performance of some of my fellow men have left much to be desired. The performance of others has been brilliant and a joy to watch. I have witnessed acts of kindness and humanity and also acts of violence and aggression.
My own performance warrants criticism. At times I have failed badly, tasted the bitterness of failure but at times - the sweet taste of success. It has been a great privilege to witness and partake in such a wonderful spectacular sharing drama, musicals and comedy with my fellow man.
Now, after seventy-five years, I realise that the last act and final curtain call cannot be very far away. I will leave the theatre quite content in mind - neither offering nor seeking forgiveness as the curtain falls I will recede into the oblivion from whence I came.

There will be no encore.

MY TIME AS A FISHERMAN IN A LOWESTOFT DRIFTER

I have already mentioned part of my history when I pedalled a Walls Ice Cream tricycle for the Summer of 1939 selling my wares - Snow Fruits, Two Penny Wafers, Snow Creams and Choc-Bars etc. - to passengers as they disembarked from the old steam chain ferry which plied from the Southwold bank of the River Blyth to the Walberswick bank. It carried two cars at a time, sometimes horse and cart, and many visitors and holidaymakers. My pitch was a good one and quite often I had to telephone my agent to bring me fresh stocks in his van.

Walberswick is an affluent village and I was often stopped and given an order for one of the Walls Ice Cream puddings or a large block of ice cream for a lunch party at one of the prominent houses in the village. I wore a blue and white striped jacket and a peaked cap. I was still only sixteen years old but looked much older. I found out by chance that I could enhance my meagre earnings if I stocked less Two Penny Wafers and held more one-shilling blocks. By mid-morning, I had run out of Two Penny Wafers and when a customer asked for one I expressed my regrets and suggested that I could divide a one-shilling block up which would amount to the same thing. This I did carefully after lifting the top of my cold box so my customer did not see and dividing my one-shilling block into seven pieces. That made me two pence profit on each block and deprived my customer of only a small amount of his entitlement.

Wages were small and I had many young lady friends who liked ice cream and being soft of heart, at the end of the week, I found my standing wage and the bonus I had earned on sales always in a state of deficiency; however I still had the benefit of my inability to count sixes and sevens!

At the end of that Summer the country was at war although little appeared to be happening. I had a commitment and had to earn a living so I wrote to the Royal Navy Enrolment Office and volunteered my services. In a matter of days I received a Rail Warrant to report to Crown Street, Ipswich for a medical inspection. The result was - as I knew it would be - I was classed as A1.

I was paid money - I forget how much - but seem to remember that it was what was termed as `taking the King's Shilling' an act which indicated your allegiance to the King and Country. In order to get this far I had advanced my age by a year, as eighteen years was the minimum age at that time for the services. Within days I received my draft papers requesting me to report to Sparrows Nest, Lowestoft - the HQ of the Naval Patrol Service on the east coast. I arranged with my Father that I would leave my cycle at the Suffolk Hotel just over the Swing Bridge at Lowestoft, from where he would collect it in a day or so. Then off I pedalled to Lowestoft (about fourteen miles) to join the Royal Navy. Young and strong then was I - the miles just floated by and I found myself pedalling through the village of Kessingland. Just ahead of me, cycling in the same direction, I saw a middle aged man, obviously a fisherman, whose pace was much slower than mine. Swinging out to overtake him he shouted out "Where the hell are you orf to boy?" Falling back beside him I explained to him that I was off to Sparrows Nest where I was to report at 2pm to join the Royal Navy. The old chap's name was Redgrave and he was known in the local fishing circles as `Redder'. He said I must be a `bloody fool' to be joining the Navy when I could earn so much more money aboard a fishing boat - and they were short of men. As it happened, he said, there was a berth aboard his boat, named `the Foresight' (I think its registered number was LT 764 but as I've already said, memories fade as the years roll by).

In short, by the time we reached Lowestoft Swing Bridge, I had abandoned the Royal Navy and had set my mind on earning a fortune as a fisherman. Time was to prove to me that Redder had stated some statistical inexactitudes and that whilst I probably did earn more money than I would have done in the Patrol Service, the gain was but very little.

Crossing the Swing Bridge we turned off left up Commercial Road to the quay where several drifters and trawlers were laid alongside. Climbing down the ladder on to the deck of `the Foresight' Redder hailed the Skipper, Stanley Turrell. "Skipper," he said, "I've got us a cook!" Hearing this, I got quite alarmed. I had never boiled an egg, never mind being a cook! They both allayed my fears by saying that all fishermen began as cooks - there were nine others in the crew and they would all help and show me what to do.

A transpired that `the Foresight' and several other drifters would set sail for Fleetwood at the weekend. The next day or two would be taken up getting the nets and gear ready - then we would put to sea just for sea trials and to have the compass adjusted. That afternoon, late, I got on my bicycle and went home to announce

The author in his wartime days

The 'Girl Pat' in Lowestoft Harbour

that I would not be a sailor after all - explaining that I was to seek my fortune from fishing. Father said nothing but I could read his thoughts. I reported aboard again the next day and did my first stint at cooking whilst the nine others of the crew set about their work. On the day of the trials I stood on the bow of the Foresight as we went through the Swing Bridge and out to sea. Lord Nelson could never have felt more important than I did. The sea was flat calm and for an hour or so it was idyllic. We tied up on the dock basin and I went home for the last time before commencing my venture to sea. In the morning I waited for the bus to take me to Southwold and on to Lowestoft. Father waited at the roadside with me and as the bus appeared he thrust something into my jacket pocket. "What's that?" I said as I was about to board the bus. "It's your fare home," said Father. "You will never stick fishing for long." By his action he had literally turned the key in the lock and ensured that I did endure the rigours ahead - there was no way in which I would have thrown in the towel after that.

I had got with me a couple of blankets and had already bought a `Donkey's Breakfast' which was a sacking palias stuffed with straw and which was to be my bedding for the trip. The morning we sailed the weather got very rough and long before we entered the straits of Dover, I was as sick as a dog. I recall looking at the chalk cliffs and weighing up the chances of making it if I went over the side. I felt absolutely dreadful until we tied up in Fleetwood when within minutes of the ships motion being stilled I felt my usual self once more.

After a short while we headed out again into the Irish Sea to catch pilchards. Then came my initiation into my duties as well as being the ships cook. The first time we `shot the nets' was late in the Winter afternoon. My job was in the rope room, which was a small area directly under the Capstan, mounted on the fore deck. Either side of the rope room was an area known as the wings and was storage for all the fish boxes. The drifter had no artificial lighting system. Navigation lights and other lights were all fuelled by a type of paraffin which we knew as Colza Oil. I believe it was smokeless fuel. The rope which was the lynchpin to the whole of the drift net exercise which covered a three-mile length of net had to be coiled with a fine precision so that it would snake out cleanly when the nets were shot over the side. The drifter had a small mast and sail on the rear deck and was termed as a mizzen sail. A slight breeze would be just enough to ensure that the drifter would have enough `way on' to keep it propelled through the water. The shoals of herrings or pilchards would be swimming close to the surface against the tide and would be caught by their gills in the mesh of the net. This task would take up to two hours. The line of nets then being set, the crew would retire to their bunks to get a few hours sleep before the Skipper's call of Work-Oh' would summon the lads to their stations to haul the nets. One end of the rope had been kept round the capstan whilst the boat drifted. Hauling the nets could take from 4-8 hours according to the weight of the catch.

The Mate would turn on the steam valve and guide the rope into the turns round the barrel of the capstan and underneath (in the rope room) my job was to coil this tarred rope into coils so neat that it was said that a marble could be bowled round the coil without any difficulty. The coil commenced on the floor of the rope room and when all the nets had been hauled, the coils were up to chest height. In order to do this, the cook, in the rope room, had his arms above his head most of the time guiding the rope into neat coils. The salt water ran down the rope and soaked the wretched cook down to the waist. Bandages around the wrist were a necessity to prevent the chafing of the wrist on the cuffs of the oilskin overalls which had to be worn. Failure to do this caused unpleasant `salt water boils' to erupt on the wrists.

Having hauled the nets, the crew would shake out the fish into fish boxes which were then topped up with ice and stowed away. The nets were also stowed away - any net which had snagged and got torn would be set aside to await repairs and replaced by another. Hauling usually commenced at dawn and if the catch was light it was completed by 8 or 9 am. If it was a heavy catch, it could go on until nearly midday.

However, it was then my task to cook breakfast which was always herring or pilchards. I had to get my buckets, select and clean a hundred fish then fry them and have them ready for when the rest of the crew had completed their tasks. Breakfast would be taken at the horseshoe shaped table under the stern deck where the living quarters were. I would have to cut up a loaf or two of bread and have jam, salt, vinegar etc. on the table ready for a hungry crewman to eat the ten fish which was the allotted ration. They ate the fish without using cutlery as a mouth organ would be played, holding the head and tail they chewed the flesh of the backbone. Breakfast over, the crew went back to their task of tidying up and repairing nets whilst I was left to wash up, scrub the table, sweep the cabin clean and keep the small open fire going all the clock round. Next I had to go down into the ice lockers and select a joint of meat for the dinner. I would then clean out the small galley stove, getting it going ready to cook the meal. Next, I would prepare the vegetables and set to work to get the meal cooked.

Here I must say that the drifter was not designed for men's comfort. The cabin was the only living quarter and behind the seat which encircled the horseshoe table, the bunks were set into the bulkhead. There were no facilities for toiletries or washing. The men slept in their clothes - jackets and trousers would be discarded and stowed in their bunks whilst they slept in their long johns, socks and woollen jerseys. They never washed or shaved unless they were going ashore - even then the ablutions were exceedingly minimal. The toilet was a wooden barrel which would be placed on the small after deck with half a bucket of water placed therein before use. After which, it was sluiced out with seawater. This was, as can well be imagined, an unpleasant and difficult thing to do in bad weather, rain or rough seas. However, the barrel was the only toilet facility on board and was used by all from the Skipper down to the lowly cook.

To the uninitiated who have never seen a drifter in turbulent weather It will be difficult to accept that this balancing act could be achieved but it was! When in port, with scores of other drifters tied up waiting to put to sea again, one had to take the barrel into the wheelhouse to gain what privacy there was to be had. Reflecting back, I cannot recall ever seeing a life jacket or first aid box aboard the drifter. What little washing and shaving that took place was managed by filling a bucket with fresh water and putting it under the steam pipe in the engine room. This could only be allowed with the blessing of the Driver. He was not called an engineer but he controlled and kept the small steam engine which propelled the drifter in good order. He was assisted by a stoker who `trimmed' the coal down into the stoke hole where he shovelled it onto the small furnace. Both these members of the crew were always smothered in coal dust so it is easy to imagine the state of personal hygiene which prevailed!

His cooking was quite primitive, no gravy or sauces would be expected, just meat and vegetables. When the meal was ready I would summon the crew - some of them may already have been resting in their bunks if their tasks were complete. The meal was a ritual. The large joint would be placed before the Skipper who would slice off what he needed. The Mate came next, followed by the

Oarsman down the line to cast off - finally the Cook. I always cooked plenty of vegetables so whilst the meat had been considerably diminished in quantity and choice, I did not starve. Apart from that, my dear old Mother - one in ten million - never failed to send me a half biscuit tin with fruit cake, rusks and buns etc. every fortnight.

After the meal was over I had to wash up then I was at liberty to rest until we shot the nets a few hours later. The drifter always smelt of fish and body odour. It would not be unkind to say that the crew were not the most hygienic but they had no means of practicing any standards of cleanliness. Old Redder, my mentor, chewed tobacco and from any distance in the cabin could eject a squirt of tobacco juice onto the hot cabin fire where it would sizzle as it hit.

During that trip, whilst we were at sea drifting, about twenty or more of us were racked with machine gun fire from a German Bomber which circled round the fleet of fishing boats. We landed our catch in Kinsale or Ballycotton and sometimes Port Erin or Douglas in the Isle of Mann.

There is so much more I could recall in the seven-month trip I did aboard `the Foresight' but I think I have adequately described the extreme hardship which was endured at that time.

The day came when, after landing our catch, the Skipper was ordered to proceed to Fleetwood for further orders. There, on the quayside, were a small group of Naval Officers who informed us that the drifter was being requisitioned by the Government for barrage balloon and minesweeping duties. We were given the choice of remaining with the boat and being automatically opted into the Royal Navy or going home. Our rank would be corresponding to our existing status. I could not imagine Skipper Stanley Turrell in the gold braid uniform of a Captain (old Redder would have been exempt anyway being over age).

I cannot remember what all the crew elected to do but some four or five of us opted out and were given rail warrants to get home. I remember the lovely Spring/early Summer weather and the sweet smell of the countryside. The joy of a good wash and clean clothes was indescribable but I had done it - Father's pound notes were still in my pocket!

I was not home for long. My eldest Brother was on a Rumanian ship, which was in Brigham Cowans Dock, South Shields, and he sent me a telegram saying that an Able Seaman was required on his ship. I replied immediately and within a few hours I was met by him at the South Shields Rail Station and was then destined to become Able Seaman aboard the 'Mirupanu' plying our trade from Blyth to London, carrying coal to fuel the huge gas works on the banks of the Thames, such as Becton.

The `Mirupanu' was quite a big vessel but very old and in some ways not much better than the little drifter I had come from. It did however have a washroom with WC but no water laid on. To get hot water, as on the `Foresight', it was necessary to put a bucket of water under the steam pipe in the engine room. However, when ashore, the Seaman's Mission or `Flying Angels' as it was known would always provide a hot bath and refreshments.

The Merchant Navy lived well - good food and plenty of it. It was a difficult time trading on the east coast. Almost without fail, dawn brought the bombers and evening brought the `E-Boats'. On one occasion the `Mirupanu' joined a convoy at Southend which consisted of 27 ships. We may have picked up 2 or 3 others in the Humber but we arrived at the Tyne with only 13 ships. All along the shallow shipping channels, mast heads and funnels poked up from the seabed. Thus it became known as ' E-Boat Alley'.

How I wish I had kept diaries of my wartime years!

MEMORIES

Whatever our station in life, be it lowly and humble or exciting and successful, there is bound to be certain incidents which, as the years pass, will be recalled in our memory. Unusual events - incidents that have caused embarrassment or may well have been humorous or perhaps a blend of both.

Whilst I have made it a hobby to recall such events as have happened to me in past years, as they come to mind, they should be recorded. Who knows? - they may be of interest and cause amusement for many people!

One such incident which I had completely forgotten has recently come to mind. This …….. it takes us back to the late fifties or early sixties happened when my company had an office base in South Mimms, Herts. It was quite near to Bignalls Corner - a very large garden / nursery complex. That area is now a huge complex of roads linking the MI with the M6 and is completely unrecognisable from what it was then

I had for some reason which I now have completely forgotten, been out with a colleague and had returned to the office later in the day. My colleague lived on the premises with his family having moved there from Suffolk. My car was parked at Ipswich Station and I was returning there by rail.

The youngest son of my colleague was a boarder at St Joseph's College, Ipswich but was home at the time and due to return to school that day. Quite naturally I was asked if I would escort the boy back to St. Joseph's. Having completed the work which I was there to do, the lad and I set off for Ipswich, my colleague having driven us to the nearest underground station en route for Liverpool Street station.

He had a couple of suitcases which I took charge of and he clung to a small wooden box no larger than a small box of cigars. It was of no interest to me to know what was inside that small box and it certainly did not cross my mind to ask.

Arriving at Liverpool Street we headed for Platform 9 and boarded the Norwich train. I put his suitcases up on the rack whilst he clung on to his small wooden box. Just inside the carriage door we sat at a table for four.

The lad took the window seat and I sat beside him. A middle aged lady sat opposite him whilst the seat opposite me remained vacant during the journey.

The suburbs of London were fast disappearing to give way to the countryside scenery. Feeling a little tired I was in a comatose state and had no doubt closed my eyes at peace with the world and my fellow travellers. The little wooden box lay on the table in front of the lad.

I recall coming to, opening my eyes and seeing the lady sitting opposite my protégé absolutely rigid with fright and a look of terror on her face. Never before had I seen anyone so utterly panic-stricken. A sideward glance at the boy alerted me to the cause of the problem. He sat there stroking a small white mouse which was clinging to the lapel of his jacket. I then understood why he carried the small wooden box so protectively.

In one swift movement I had the mouse off his lapel and back in the box with the lid firmly in place. A fatherly talk then ensued when I attempted to explain to him that not everyone was fond of mice - particularly elderly ladies! I gathered that he had purchased the mouse from a school friend who had let him have it cheap because he knew it would be going to a `good home'. It cost him one shilling and sixpence.

The lady soon recovered her composure and accepted my sincere apologies for the actions of an unthinking ten-year-old boy. I delivered him, his luggage and his mouse to St Joseph's College and have never heard more of the episode or been reminded of it since.

THE EAST ANGLIAN HERRING FISHING INDUSTRY AND A REMARKABLE STORY OF THE 'GIRL PAT'

The Motor Vessel "Girl Pat"

Built by:	*Geo. Overy, Lowestoft*
Launched:	*16 April 1935*
Length:	*65'*
Beam:	*19'*
Draught:	*$10^1 6^{11}$*
Knots:	*9.63*
Range	*1897 nautical miles*
Engine:	*125 BHP Atlas Polar Diesel*

Registered at Lloyds, London
Official Reg. No. 162904 - GY 176
Timber Construction - 19 tons net, approx. 34 tons gross

Built for The Marstrand Fishing Company, Grimsby

East Anglia is a large region - supported mainly from agricultural and maritime trades. It's people are a tough, hardened race who have had to work their way thro' life. It would not be far off the mark to say that the region has been considered to be one of the nation "s most deprived areas. Because of it's long coastline, stretching from The Wash south to the Thames Estuary, it is natural that so many East Anglians earned a living from the sea and that the agricultural industries beyond the coastline also gained an advantage from the seafarers' activities.

The main ports of Hull, Grimsby, Kings Lynn, Yarmouth and Lowestoft were, at the turn of the century, fully employed in the fishing industry making a great contribution to the nation's larder. Trawlers ventured out into the North Sea trawling the waters almost up to the Arctic Circle arriving home laden with cod, haddock, skate and all species of deep-water fish. During the herring season as the vast shoals of herrings moved south down the coastline, the drifters with their great expanse of nets literally swept the sea of these tasty and nutritious fish.

Year after year the routine was the same and the harbours would be jammed packed with the small steam driven vessels of local registration together with those of the northern fleet which were following the herrings south as far as the Cornish coast. Each day the fish docks in East Anglian ports were a hive of industry. The fish docks would be literally packed out with the herring drifters, the crew busily offloading their catch in order to put to sea again in quest of the shoals of herrings which were their only livelihood.

The dockside was piled high with boxes and barrels of these silvery fish, the air was pervaded with the smell of fish, salt and tanning liquids. Lassies from Lerwick and the northern areas were there gutting the fish - they were so quick with their sharp knives and without exception they all sported finger bandages where they had misjudged their distance.

For reasons unknown, it appears that the Harvest of the North Sea has always been sold by the 'cran'. This was a volume rather than a weight. A 'cran' was approximately a thousand herring and were measured in strong wicker baskets very similar to the 'bushel skep' which is used in the agricultural industry. A 'skepful' of fish was indeed a 'cran'. Lifted from the drifter fish hold, they were swung up onto the dockside to be packed in boxes of approximately 4'x2'x8" deep or barrels packed with ice or salt and sent off all over the country.

Not only deep sea drifters sought out the herring shoals but along the coast small boats of not more that 20 feet in length, went out daily in search of the fish which swam in the waters which were much too shallow for the drifters. They used a much shorter length of net but managed to come ashore at times loaded to the gunwales with fish. In the case of the 'Longshore' men, they sold their catch by the 'Longhundred'. This was in fact 132 fish. A tarpaulin would be spread out beside the boat when it was winched up the beach above the high tide mark and the fish would then be shaken from the nets onto the tarpaulin and counted out into boxes which would then be transported to the nearest fish market and on to the consumer.

So there were two methods of selling the catches of herrings - obviously a longstanding tradition which was carried on right up to the demise of the herring trade just after the last World War. Many villages along the coastline were populated by 'Longshore' fishermen, many have survived to this present day. Some were lucky to have a small river outlet to the sea - others just put to sea from the beach. Obviously the weather played a big part in their fortunes and often they were unable to put to sea because of weather conditions. They also fished for cod, skate, whiting, etc. when the herrings had moved south of their destination - a 'Longshore' boat had only a 20 mile range.

There were times in the early days when the market demand fell off and the fish were not all required for human consumption was then that the vast quantities of fish were processed into fish manure greatly benefiting the agricultural industry. This was short-lived when the large frozen food companies such as Bird Eye frozen foods got to grips with the fish markets and from then on very little was wasted.

East Anglia has certainly bred some extraordinary characters and it leaves no doubt that because of our long coastline and maritime connections many of them were seamen. Very few people would admit to having no knowledge of East Anglia's most famous son of the sea - Admiral Lord Horatio Nelson. How many Anglians would remember the name of Skipper Dod Orsborne - a Grimsby trawler skipper whose incredible actions in absconding in a chartered trawler together with his crew of three men and disappearing from the sight of the world from the time they left

The crew being arrested

Dod Osbourne, his wife and his brother

Grimsby until they were apprehended in Georgetown, Guyana? The only navigational assistance that Dod Orsborne had was a folding atlas of the world, which cost just sixpence plus a 12" ruler and a pencil, a remarkable feat of seamanship.

When the idea of absconding with the 'Girl Pat' entered his head is anybody's guess. He discussed it with his crew - Jim Orsborne (his brother), Howard Stephen and Hector Harris. There was a fifth person, the ship's engineer, who for some reason Dod did not want as a participant in his scheme. Therefore he was put ashore before the 'Girl Pat' left territorial waters.

It was on 14 April 1936 when they slipped out of Grimsby setting off on this remarkable voyage. They headed south and had to cross the Bay of Biscay to reach the Spanish coast. This in itself was a nightmare. The 'Girl Pat' was tossed about but able to make headway past large ships which were battened down against the bad weather could only manage to steam at half speed. They reached the coast of Spain off Corcubion and within hours the telegraphs and submarine cable were humming with excited messages. This was the first intimation that Dod and his crew had to the effect that the escapade of the 'Girl Pat' was now international news. There they heard that, in the eyes of the world, Dod Orsborne was in command of a pirate ship with millions of pounds of gold bullion aboard, prowling the seas and plundering ships.

Moored in the small harbour, it was not long before a posse of Spanish police appeared very highly excited. Gathering on the dock side was a large crowd of local inhabitants. They had all read or heard of this vessel by newspapers and radio.

The police fired questions at Dod, neither side being able to understand what was being said. They demanded to see the ship's papers to which Dod obliged - holding them upside down. The senior policeman made copious notes. Then they searched the ship from top to bottom and seemed satisfied that all was in order. Just then a launch came alongside with two men in plain clothes - Harbour Officials. One could manage a little English and told Dod that he would be fined 100 pesetas. Dod explained that he was there for engine repairs and the man's attitude changed immediately - he would not enforce the fine!

Then the port doctor arrived and Dod requested to see or speak to a Lloyd's agent which the doctor said he would arrange the next morning. In the meantime, would Dod and his crew like to go ashore with him? This they gladly accepted and at the cafe where they were taken they rapidly sank a few bottles of wine and appeased their appetites before returning to the 'Girl Pat'.

The next morning another man came on board saying he was a Lloyds agent (it proved otherwise in the end) and Dod was able to get through to him what was required to fix the engine. It was several days and several attempts later by different mechanics before the engine was running sweetly again. Then they quietly slipped out of the harbour with no fuss and sailed away from Corcubion.

Heading south under a sultry sun, the 'Girl Pat' was enroute for Africa. Thoughts went through Dod's mind that he may never see his wife and family again. They just ate and slept, played cards, as the `Girl Pat' glided over sun-drenched seas. Seeing a group of small islands and studying his sixpenny atlas, Dod was sure they were just off the Canaries. Sure enough it was not long before the snow-capped mountains of Tenerife came into view.

During the voyage Dod and his men had set about painting their ship and making more sails in case they ran out of fuel. They now had a clean, tidy, white painted ship completely different to the grey painted and patched red leaded vessel that had left Grimsby a few weeks prior.

Calling at one of the small islands, they managed to row ashore and obtain supplies of food and water. This procedure took place many times before their voyage came to any end. Many strange events took place - all far too numerous to record here. They had to beg for food from passing ships and in one case were refused. Many days were spent grounded on a sand bank at least 60 miles from the nearest land. The waters were infested with sharks. Often they thought that the 'Girl Pat' was doomed. Food had reduced to just enough for 24 hours so Dod had to enforce a strict rationing - there appeared to be no help available. Sick with hunger and depression they rowed out with an anchor and wire hawser and were able to winch their way forward and get off the sand bank - only to ground on another a few minutes later. However, they eventually made it.

Many unpleasant experiences and deprivations were suffered before the ship was detained and they were arrested in Georgetown - far too many to describe in this short appraisal of the remarkable achievement of Skipper Dod Orsborne and his crew. From the day they left Grimsby to the time they arrived back in London to face the music, more than six months had elapsed.

Dod Osbourne and his brother

The 'Girl Pat'

Their actions were, in the eyes of the law, a criminal
offence. Dod and his men made international news and
Dod was guilty of stealing a drifter. Whatever his objective
was never really disclosed other than when he was
scanning over his sixpenny atlas, seeing all the
names of foreign ports, he just had an urge to visit them and said to
himself "Why not?"
He proved to be a brilliant seaman and leader of men. He was able
to give a good account of himself in the boxing ring. Fishing for a
living was a hard life with poor financial returns and did he think
that he could find gold in these far away lands? Did he realise that
if he survived the voyage he would eventually had to answer for
his misdeeds? Had the thought occurred to him that after being
hailed as an international object of interest, he could make easy
money by selling his story, which I think he did to the Sunday
newspaper 'The People', or what he might achieve by writing a
book about his adventures?
We have now put some 63 years between the time he embarked on
his remarkable voyage and the present time so it is unlikely that the
world will even know why he really did it. His wife and family -
were they part of the act and even if they were in the know they
must have been sick with worry? How did they exist for six
months with no money coming into the household?
Dod and his brother, Jim, were brought back to the UK from
Georgetown after the 'Girl Pat' had been detained by the port
authority. They appeared at Bow Street Police Court on an
indictment of two charges alleging they had conspired with
persons unknown to steal the motor vessel 'Girl Pat', valued at
£3,600, being the property of the Marstrand Fishing Company
within British territorial waters on or about 4 April 1936. They
were ordered to appear at the London Central Criminal Court on
19 October 1936 before Mr Justice Singleton who found them both
to be guilty, awarding Dod with 18 months hard labour and his
brother, Jim, 12 months.
When the dust had all settled down and the two brothers were
serving their sentences in prison, international affairs were far from
settled. Within a few month of Dod's release the country was at
war. It is believed that Dod enrolled in the Royal Naval Patrol
Service and was given the rank of Captain commanding a fishing
vessel which has been converted for minesweeping. It appears that

the 'Girl Pat' was brought back to the UK and was also sequested by the Royal Navy for naval duties.

In conclusion there is no doubt that Dod Osborne committed an offence in the eyes of the law. It did show, however, that he and his crew were of the same ilk, which made Britain the great nation, which she is. It proved that Dod was a brilliant seaman and leader of men, just as Horatio Nelson was. Perhaps this is an unfair equation but who would deny that a similar characteristic existed in both men?

Has Grimsby failed to recognise a golden opportunity to erect a small plague to one of it's outstanding sons - a man who sailed a small fishing vessel from Grimsby to Georgetown on a shoe string with just a sixpenny pocket atlas and a 12 inch ruler apart form unlimited courage and a stout heart!

LIFE ON THE OCEAN WAVE

Geography was never my best subject! Beyond the East Anglia boundaries, I realized that all sorts of life existed but I never knew where in the world Peru, Chile and Argentina could be found - would it be North, East, South or West? Come to that, I really do not know and cannot remember if ever I excelled at any subject but I know that I never achieved any academic standard at school and not many people did in the 1930's, education was rather basic in those days. I attended the council school at Wenhaston and it would be misleading if I suggested I was a pupil, a rebel would be much nearer the mark. During geography lessons, sitting at my desk I recall being shown an illustrated geography book, the subject for the lesson that day was a place I had never heard of before and had never bothered to find out its position in the world. After all I never dreamed that I would have the opportunity or inclination to visit anywhere outside East Anglia and had no means of getting there if I did! My dear old dad had bought me a new Hercules bicycle for the sum of three pounds seventeen shillings and sixpence from John O'Neil's cycle shop in Halesworth - a shop I was greatly attracted to, the smell of new cycles all lined up with three speed gears - dynamo lighting plus other goods would give me several hours enjoyment.

My Hercules cycle was the only means of transport I had at that time. It got me to school, to the beach at Walberswick and Dunwich, to the woods and fields where my heart was and where I found tremendous enjoyment as a young lad. It would have been little help to me had I have expanded my interest geographically into other spheres. So it transpired that I did not take advantage of my time at school and had little interest in the outside world. Yet here I am at the age of seventy-nine on a cold wet miserable January day being driven to Southampton to embark on a magnificent cruise ship, the "Black Watch", which would be my only abode for the next sixty-nine days, visiting many far away places which as a young lad I had abandoned interest in. In fact we did travel almost to the southern ocean at the bottom of the world, verging the South Pole. It was an adventure which embraced sixteen countries and twenty-three different points of call in a total mileage of twenty one thousand and five hundred miles.

Arriving at Southampton we reported as instructed to a Hotel nearer the dock area. Luggage was clearly labelled and it was whisked away smartly.

The next time we saw it was safe in the cabin, which had been allocated to us. Registration was simple after which it was time to relax, enjoy a coffee and meet other people. We were all in a large room and my wife was already meeting many old shipmates we had cruised with before. Looking around I noticed that almost without exception the room was full of senior citizens, I would estimate the average age was sixty five to seventy years. Some were infirm requiring the aid of walking sticks and other devices. There were a couple of wheelchairs (for the uninitiated) - Cruise Ships are well equipped with lifts to each deck making it possible for any person to enjoy a voyage even if they are bound to a wheelchair. Modern ships are fitted with stabilisers which reduce movement caused by the waves considerably, so when in rough weather the ship is quite steady.

Sitting there, taking stock of my new shipmates, I gained an opinion that couples all had a sound "togetherness", they helped each other, the gentlemen would fetch a cup of coffee for his wife, she would rummage in her bag and produce a pill or tablet for him. They held hands and engaged in low voiced conversation - they were indeed a "unit" bound together by several years of affection and respect. This, bond of unity remained throughout the voyage, holding each other's hand as they walked around the shop. They showed care and concern for each other's safety and comfort. They made many friends with others of the same ilk. Photographs of grandchildren and family were shown around with pride. No doubt during their many years they had raised a family now long since flown the nest. Now with not many pages left in the book they had taken the action and chose a cruise to remember and what a wise decision it was -sixty nine days of sheer luxury and just like myself - they were to see sights and places they never thought they would see. Undoubted they had saved a bit in their working years. Perhaps moved into a smaller house and gained a bit of capital. Maybe a golden handshake or a pension sum - an insurance policy had matured or whatever. No doubt their children encouraged them in making the decision- saying, "go on enjoy your remaining years, we can manage, spend your money - its what you have worked for all these years".

But what will happen in future years - where will the people come from who will fill the cruise ships? With such a large dependency on social security together with the advent of the modern age ten-day

A cruising ship in a Norwegian fiord.

*Arthur and his wife Margaret about to go ashore
to see what the Falklands had to offer.
A visit not to be forgotten*

marriages which will never contribute to the future - and the equally unsound foundation of the so-called "partnerships" which can be very fragile, the future does not look good. There is so much to be said for the good old-fashioned way of life, the bond of sound marriage and its product - "togetherness". Here I must put reader's minds at rest cruising is not expensive, it is very good value for money. It almost relates to the claim of the Railways in the 1930s who claimed they could transport passengers for "one penny a mile". I must get back to where I left you in the hotel at Southampton. Buses arrived and transported us to the dockside where the sleek and gleaming white "Black Watch" awaited our arrival. Time was now getting on and after locating your cabin and unpacking your luggage it is time for a much-needed reviving drink at the bar before taking dinner in the restaurant and so to bed.

Waking up the next morning we found ourselves at sea heading south for the far away places that we never dreamed we would ever see. Plenty of time now to explore the ship and get your bearings. Between decks, amidships is the reception desk, which is always open to assist passengers. All you need to do is ask - they will assist you. You will meet many people during the voyage and make may new friends. Couples who cruise regularly often book next years cruise in advance taking advantage of early booking discounts. There is no need for anybody thinking of taking a cruise to be concerned about anything - every facility possible is provided and catered for. First, healthwise, there is a small hospital - three or four beds - staffed by a doctor and two or three qualified nurses. Every cabin has a telephone which will get you contacted to any of the cabins on the ship - or any of the admin offices. You can also contact the outside world from your cabin. You can send a fax or e-mail from the ship as you can also receive them

The cuisine on board is unimaginable. Prepared by the best chefs it is presented beautifully. Variety is great and of the highest quality. Should you need a special diet or anything you cannot see on the menu your waiter will arrange everything for you if warned in advance. It will not cause them any problem. There are several bars aboard the ship and bar staff move around the decks and will fetch any drink should you fancy a small libation. What is there to do all day long? You will be surprised. Every night the next days programme is put in your cabin. This is a timed programme of the ships events. There will be talks, lectures, handicraft classes, darts, whist, bridge, quiz programmes etc, etc. Each and every day is mapped out with interesting events. There are grand pianos in some of the ships lounges with professional pianists to entertain you most. Most evenings there is a show with a cast of singers and comedians - conjurers etc, backed up by the "Black Watch Band". All good acts who play the cruise ships as others play the clubs and seaside theatres home.

The day before the ship reaches a foreign port, a port talk is given and slides are shown illustrating what you may expect to find there. The talk gives advice on currency - places of interest to see - advise on what merchandise is worth buying etc, etc. The ship has organised tours available at every port which can be pre booked before the day of arrival. Alternatively, couples will have made many friends by this time and groups of four or six can hire a taxi and do their own thing. Taxis will be waiting at the dockside ready for you. On a cruise, unexpected pleasures will turn up. Schools of dolphins are often sighted - the occasional huge whale can be seen leaping clear of the sea to create a great splash, flying fish are often seen skimming the water in great numbers.

At the age of 79 on this particular cruise I am enjoying it immensely and learning a lot, of which I should have learned at school. We are cruising to the bottom of the world, rounding Cape Horn, the dreaded area for sailors in the old windjammer days, skirting the southern ocean, sailing through the Beagle Channel into the Chilean Fjords and on to the Atlantic Ocean through the Panama Canal starting the homeward journey - still some ten thousand miles away from home. In one Fjord there is a glacier reputed to be the largest in that part of the world. The suns rays give it a vivid tinge of blue. Stopping the ship - tenders were lowered and passengers taken right up to the foot of the huge amount of ice. We were blessed with an excellent friendly captain determined that we should enjoy the voyage to the full. Two crewmembers took pick axes and buckets and they brought these back to the ship full of ice. The captain then arranged for bottles of Scotch to be provided and passengers were able to enjoy "scotch on the rocks". The ice was estimated to be between five hundred thousand and one million years old!! What an experience for such as me who showed no interest in geography in my school days. Anybody who reads my tale of cruising and description of what it is really like and are thinking about making such a venture I say without hesitation - delay no longer. Get in touch with a travel agent or direct to the shipping line - this cruise line is based at the White House Estate in Ipswich. As I have just completed my fifth voyage on the "Black Watch" I can speak from experience. Old age is to be enjoyed as much as possible. Do not concern yourself at being thought of as spending your children's inheritance. Should you be fortunate to have a works pension and perhaps a bit in the bank together with your old age pension most of you can achieve your ambitions. It cost nothing over your initial payment whilst aboard ship except what you spend over the bar and whilst ashore. For your comfort and safety, the "Black Watch" employs three hundred and thirty staff to care for eight hundred or so passengers. Each of whom is dedicated to his or her job. Any complaints will be dealt with sympathetically.

So - delay no longer.   "See you on the next cruise".

WARTIME MEMORIES

From 1939 to 1945 our towns and cities were bristling with uniformed men and women. Men of different Services - of different nationalities, all with a sense of purpose - get on with the War so we can all go back to our peaceful way of living. The country seethed with the fighting forces - on their way in transit or on leave. The W.V.S. and other good organisations set up stalls in every quarter - railway stations or wherever so every serving man or woman could get a good hot cup of tea and a bun to help them on their journey. Last but certainly not least our good old Sally Army was there to serve and help whatever the weather, for twenty-four hours a day.

Probably very few people gave thought to the great contribution these good people gave to the War Effort. Servicemen, feeling down hearted at having to leave his wife and family - tired from long train journeys - tied to a difficult timetable to report back to his unit would be welcomed with a cheerful smile, words of comfort and refreshments.

Those were the days when trains were packed tight with serving personnel, some were lucky enough to get a seat, many others not so lucky. Corridors of trains were packed with them, sitting on suitcases, on kit-bags, trying to snatch a little sleep between the times when their travelling companions wished to edge past to get to the toilet at the end of the corridor. Having travelled many times in these conditions I do not recall a single incident where tempers became frayed or hard words said. No doubt, suffering hardship with fellow men caused many a good friendship to be created.

Intermingled with these seething masses were a vast number of men - unnoticed and unrecognised by the general public - who were gallantly adding their contribution to the War effort. It would not be incorrect to suggest that these men were not and never have been acclaimed for what they did to serve the country. They were attired in civilian clothes, usually dark in colour with a roll neck jumper rather than a collar and tie. They had not sworn allegiance to the King and Country. Neither had they need to, they were following their normal profession and were fiercely patriotic with deep national pride.

Classed as civilians they were men of the Merchant Navy. Their only means of identification was a small silver badge worn in the lapel, a wreath of leaves surrounding the letters M.N., together with their special identity card which bore all their personal details and their finger prints - just enough details to identify a body if found to be floating at sea. Officers did have a uniform similar to that of the Royal Navy. I suppose they had to be recognised apart from the crew because they had to work closely with the Royal Navy. There was a briefing before any convoy left port. The Navy would plan and guide the convoy, placing a senior Officer aboard "Commodore Ship" and was to lead the other ships to their destination.

Crew members - seamen and firemen (the firemen were thus named because they stoked the steam boilers which gave the ship its means of propulsion) had little or few disciplines to follow. Every man had to register with the Shipping Pool and his progress was monitored by them. There was a standard set for holidays, once a holiday or leave had expired a man was expected to either rejoin his ship or report to the Shipping Pool from where he would be directed to join his next vessel. He had no choice to make – he was directed - it could be to a vessel which was programmed for Arctic Convoy - the Atlantic or the beleaguered Island of Malta. Despite the loss of thousands of tons of British Shipping this island fortress needed food and supplies. This was achieved by the unending effort of the Merchant Navy.

Being civilians, Merchant Seamen were employed by the Ships Owner, not the Government, which had all the shipping on charter. In the event of a ship being sunk by enemy action the crew's pay would cease from the time the ship went down. Those fortunate enough to get away in the lifeboats and were eventually picked up and brought back to these shores would receive a statutory three weeks survivors' leave before having to report back to the Shipping Pool to be allocated to another ship. During the time they were on Survivor's Leave and on the Pool list for drafting, they got their normal pay which I suppose was paid from Government funds. There was none of the present day 'counselling' - no sympathy except from those who were nearest and dearest, in fact little or no financial help. A fund did exist where a Seaman could get financial help to replace his personal belongings which had finished up in "Davey Jones' locker". Consequently many men filed up a ship's gangway to sign on for his next voyage and would immediately request - and would be given - a "sub" to be deducted from their first month's pay. Sea Farers were always paid monthly which in turn applied to any allotment he wished to make either to wife or parents. All seaman - Naval or Merchantmen were greatly supported by the tireless women of this country who continually made woollen jumpers, socks, hats and mittens. These ladies would buy the wool or unravel old garments to knit these comforts for the men. These were usually sent to a collection depot and then onwards to the Mission to Seamen where the Padre would in his discretion issue them out to the many men who sought warmth and comfort of the Mission better known as the "Flying Angel".

As in every walk of life, there were the small numbers of seamen who would inevitably abuse this wonderful charity. They were the hard drinking types whose ambitions appeared to be to just live for the day only and whilst doing so consume as much alcohol as time and money would allow. Because of these few men, many of the comforts so kindly given by the ladies, found their way into the dockside public houses where they were sold for cash to buy drinks. Fortunately this was a minority and the greater number of men who were standing on duty on the ships' bridge, punching their way through the North Sea in the depth of Winter would keep warm and were eternally grateful to the ladies of Britain who never failed to supply these comforts.

It was my privilege to be one of these men. There were many dark and difficult unpleasant times - many heartaches to bear, but there were also some wonderful times as well. At the age of twenty I had already two years' experience in trading, up and clown the East Coast - from London to Blyth in Northumberland. This shipping lane was given the name tag of "E Boat Alley". Around 1942 convoys were attacked every evening as darkness fell by "E Boats" and every morning at daybreak by dive-bombers. At one time I was in a convoy which left the Thames with twenty-seven ships - we arrived in the Tyne with thirteen.

For a long time I sailed from London to the Tyne where our ship would be loaded at a small quay on the left bank of the river - at a small town named Dunston. There we found our Northern friends so hospitable that it was overwhelming. Mostly of mining families, these good people would find the means and ingredients to throw regular parties at their modest houses. They were so good hearted and shared all they had with those not so fortunate. The Seaman's

Mission was always ready to welcome a seaman, with food and drink always on offer. Weekly dances were held and if I was lucky to be in port at the time I could be sure of a warm and friendly reception. Many romances ensued from these evenings.

However daylight would follow and the ship would head out of the Tyne, past the Black Middens - an outcrop of rock in the mouth of the Tyne, out into the rolling sea where it would converge with other ships and join the convoy, which was bound for London or the Channel Ports. These convoys would be preceded by Mine Sweepers - small wooden vessels converted from fishing drifters. Sweepers would clear the narrow channel which the convoy had to navigate. The enemy disrupted our normal routine when they introduced the magnetic mine. This was a mine which was triggered off by the magnetic force of several thousand tons of steel passing over it. However our scientists quickly found a way of combating this. Every ship was fitted with a de-gauzing system which was a simple electric circuit round the ship which neutralised the magnetic forces.

In spite of the difficult times in the mid-war period there was always a time when humour and light heartiness took over. Most village people of that time kept a sporting gun and it was by this that they were able to feed the family with rabbit and wild fowl meat. Perhaps the occasional pheasant came their way also. Therefore when I got home on leave, I spent a lot of my time shooting. In 1944, I volunteered for "Special Services" and on D-Day, I found myself anchored off the beach at Arromanches in Normandy at 11.30am, the ship loaded with supplies and armaments for our forces as they went ashore.

This cargo was unloaded by military personnel into landing barges and D.U.K.S. which plied from ship to shore. As a young fearless and rather stupid seaman I got one of the D.U.K.S. drivers to get me ashore so I could look around the town. Heavy fighting was still going on all around - there ware land mines everywhere, but I was lucky to come away unscathed.

So I was able to explore the vast concrete gun emplacements and defence the enemy had constructed. It was in one of these bunkers that I came across boxes of black 12 bore cartridges filled with what look like buck shot. Just the thing - I thought to myself, for duck shooting when I get home on leave! Several boxes of these cartridges found their way back on board the "Empire Ness" and eventually to Blythburgh.

On my next leave as daylight was fading I prepared to go flighting for duck on the marshes east of the village. Going through the village I caught up with one of the local men who was bent on the same mission as I was so we walked on together. Before we got to our stand I gave him a handful of my newly acquired German cartridges. We stood some sixty yards apart, waiting for the flights of duck as they came inland to feed. There was not much about and it was nearly dark when I heard a flight of Widgeon approaching - directly over where my colleague was standing. Then I heard this huge explosion and saw an orange coloured flame leap into the sky and instinctively knew that he had used one of those cartridges. The echo of the bang rolled away along the woods and all fell quiet. Calling him by name, I got no answer. Becoming concerned I walked over to where he was silhouetted in the darkness. He was holding the butt of his gun and the barrels were protruding from the mud a few feet away. He was shaking like an aspen leaf but luckily, completely unhurt.

Then he spoke in his strong Suffolk dialect. "Boy" he said, "I've brook my gun!" Stupidly I had failed to realise that his gun was probably the same gun that his father had used before him and was probably unsafe using an ordinary cartridge - let alone one of my German block busters. Looking back I have often thought how stupid I was, but then - at the age of twenty-three perhaps I could be forgiven.

THE FUNNY SIDE OF IT

During the war villages became a very tight knit community. My father was regarded by the villagers as being a person to whom they could turn for advice and help. He was active on the Parish Council and later moved into the politics of County Council work. He was a self-taught person of elementary education only but finished his days as an Alderman of the County.

He often had visits from strangers and he would receive them in our "front room" as it was known then. We all knew that he had a special task to carry out should the Germans invade our shores. He never mentioned what his special duties were but I strongly suspected that he was one of a special team chosen to confuse and disrupt the enemy should they have occupied the village - such as detonate the charges already put in place in the concrete piers supporting the river bridge just north of Blythburgh village. Therefore it was only natural that on dark winter nights when the enemy bombers droned overhead he would put on his special constable's gear and leave the house. Mostly he accompanied the village constable whose house was next to ours on the outside of the village.

Father loved a good joke and had a great sense of humour. One particular evening on such a night as the bombers droned high overhead and the search lights sited on Henham Park stabbed the sky with their penetrating beams, he and the Constable stood on the Post Office corner. Keeping his voice low as if being afraid of the enemy overhearing him the village Constable said "Blast George - they're up a rum depth!"

WOT! NO PILOT?

It was well on towards the end of the war that I first saw one.
At the time I was on a ship named the Empire Ness and we lay in
King George V Dock in London loading supplies to take to our
Armed Forces as they pushed their way through to Germany and
ultimate victory.

Whilst lying at anchor or on moorings all ships are safe - guarded at
night by the appointment of one of the crew as the night watchman.
This meant that one had to walk around the ship several times in the
hours of darkness and check that mooring ropes were in order and
that the ship was not dragging its anchor. It was also the night
watchman's duty to see all the crew back aboard safely after an
evening out. Whilst at the dockside a companion way (set of stairs)
was tied into position to allow men to negotiate their way safely on
and off the ship.

The crew would return late in the evening and "turn in" - the nautical
term for going to bed. From that time the ship fell silent and the night
watchman would enjoy his supper and remain vigilant until daylight
broke.

However, King George V Dock being on the side of Thames in the
East End of London there was never any peace. Searchlights pierced
the night sky and the bombers droned overhead. Red reflections in
the sky pinpointed fires all around the City and the constant bomb
explosions shattered the night air.

This particular evening it was my turn as night watchman. I have
regretted many times since that I never kept a diary to refer to for
dates of the experiences that befell me almost daily.

However, I was leaning against the ship's rail looking down river at
the night sky when I sensed a low flying plane approaching. As it
appeared in view I noted that it had a light or glow at the rear of the
fuselage.

The anti aircraft guns from Southend to the City had all fired at this
aircraft as it headed towards the densely populated area of the East
End.

I saw it pass through three Box Barrages (multi-barrelled guns firing
salvoes of twenty -thirty shells in one burst). The plane never
deviated - it carried on a straight course up river. I knew then that I
had seen a plane with no pilot on board - no human could have flown
through that barrage without deviating course.

I called the crew at 7am and fetched their breakfast from the galley. Telling them of what I had seen in the early hours, they all laughed at my statement, suggesting I had dropped off to sleep and dreamt of this - or that I had been drinking too much!

At 10am the next morning the whole dock was a hive of activity. Cranes were swinging from dock and ships with huge cargoes all over the dock. A transit shed to our left was feeding hundreds of troops through to a troop carrying vessel moored close by.

Then it happened - one of the pilot-less planes I had seen earlier approached - its engines cut out and it dived into the dock within a hundred feet of our ships, then another followed in quick succession followed by many more. One fell on the transit shed killing scores of the embarking soldiers. Pandemonium broke out as these planes rained down on the London Dock area.

I had witnessed the first Doodlebug that crashed on London - it was the first time I had ever seen one but most certainly was not the last!

v.z.w. TALBOT HOUSE van Poperinge
Talbot House
Gasthuisstraat 43
B - 8970 Poperinge
Belgium
Tel. + 32 57 33 32 28

Poperinge, 1999-12-02

Mr. Arthur CLARKE
Windyacres
Waldringfield
WOODBRIDGE
GB- SUFFOLK IP12 4PT
GREAT BRITAIN

Dear Mr. Clarke,

Many greetings from 'The Old White House in Pops' and I hope that you are keeping well.

Please accept my apologies for my belated reply to your most welcome letter dated 18th November. Traditionally I take my holidays from the 15th till the 30th November, hence this great delay.

I am delighted with all the information you have sent me and I really appreciate all the work you haven done for us. Be sure we will do some research and who knows, the name of your uncle might show up in our archives some day - one never knows. Of course, we will contact you immediately when that happens !

It is for me heartwarming to realize that there are people like you who treasure and respect the memory of a relative who became a victim of the Great War and I thank you again very much for the information that you sent me.

With all best wishes for a happy, prosperous and healthy 2000 !

Yours sincerely,

Jacques Ryckebosch

Windyacres
Waldringfield
Woodbridge
Suffolk
IP12 4PT

01473-736-606
Tel: Waldringfield 606

18 November 1999

<u>For the attention of Jaques Ryckerbosch</u>

Talbot House
Gasthuistraat 43
B8970
POPERINGHE
BELGIUM

Dear Friend

You will no doubt recall about four weeks ago you arranged with my daughter to have a conducted tour of Talbot House for our coach party. There were 46 members of our party and without exception each one of us were greatly impressed by the welcome you gave and above all, the clear and precise discussions we had and the film display which you so aptly talked through.

At that meeting I promised you that I would send you letters written by my uncle to my mother before he was killed in 1918. I had some time ago photographed the letters because being written in pencil and worn where the paper was folded, plus the fact that a photocopy would be clearer, it seemed prudent to do.

I have had the letters typed to make them easier to read and given a short note on my uncle's life. I hope you will accept these and display them in Talbot House. Unfortunately I have mislaid the original pencil written letters but as soon as I locate them I will send them on to you.

Again, many thanks for giving my daughter and her party such an entertaining tour and I wish you every success in the future.

Yours sincerely

Arthur Clarke

PRIVATE ARTHUR HATCHER

Arthur Hatcher was the son of a Rabbit Warrener residing on the Fen, a border of land adjoining an expanse of marshland bordering the North Sea, at Blythburgh in Suffolk The family were poor but hard working. A family of five, my mother was the eldest and she and Arthur were extremely close.

Probably because of the lack of work and fired by loyalty and the exuberance of youth, Arthur answered the nation's call and volunteered to join the army. As far as I am aware, he only wrote two letters before he was killed in 1918. These I found in my mother's possessions after she died some twenty years ago. The original were written in pencil and no doubt over the years, Mother read them time and again - consequently they are not in good shape, coming apart where the paper was folded.

Arthur's body was never officially identified but in a military cemetery quite near Albert in France, a headstone on a grave is inscribed 'Believed to be Private Arthur Hatcher, Norfolk Regiment'.

I was born in 1922, a year after Mother married, and because of her closeness to her brother I was named after him. Mother never really accepted his death, I believe she lived and died with a broken heart.

***Arthur Hatcher's grave in the
Cemetery near Albert in France***

From: Private Arthur Hatcher
        24851 `A' Company
        1st Norfolk Regiment
        BEF
        FRANCE

My dear Sister

Just a line to let you know I have arrived quite safe somewhere in France. I must not say where but I am a long way off the firing line although I just can't say. I just say I will be at the Front when this letter reaches you. I am glad to say that I like being here, we don't have to work so hard - about 4 hours a day and sleep the rest. We have some good food so you need not worry about me. I am quite happy and long to reach the firing line so I can see what it is like. I hope it will soon be over so we can all be happy once more. Still I hope to meet you again before long, I just say I shall be finding it a bit rough before I see you again, still I don't feel shaky a bit. I keep waiting for the order to go up to the firing line. The French trains don't go so fast as ours, they are rough riding inside, it's no use worrying about it I shall make the best of it when I go up to the line. Well, dear Sister I hope May, dear, is going alright - tell her not to worry, the war won't last forever.

Well - I went through London, I never thought I should go through London, it is a big place I can tell you. I had a lovely ride through France, I have enjoyed myself very much up to the present.

Well dear Sister, I don't think I have got much more news this time so I will bring this to a close with my best love and good luck to you both.

From your ever loving Brother,

Arthur
XXXXXXXXX

From: Private Arthur Hatcher 24851
          `A' Company
          1st Norfolk Regiment
          BEF
          FRANCE

My dear Sister

Just a line to let you know I am alright and I hope you are the same.
You look alright in the photo. I took them into the trenches when I
went in so you have been `under fire'. My word it is a rough place
up there. I was in one day and two nights and there are the worst -
still I got through that lot quite safe and I hope it won't be long
before it is all over. I expect the Germans are getting tired of it. I
hope so anyhow I am longing to see you all again. There is not
a lot of life out here, it is strange to me. Tell me of England before
France. I haven't come across anybody I know yet whether I shall
do, I hope so. I hope Bertie Wilson is alright as I have not written
to him yet. I haven't had time - I hope he is still on Leiston Works.
If you see him tell him I have been out and I am going on alright.

I don't think this war will last much longer, I hope not. Well, dear I
don't know whether you have sent a letter off since you got my
other, if you have I have not got it, this is August 4th - I expect
they get lost on the way coming all that way and us keep moving
about they get lost so we don't get them - still I will write to you
when I get the chance as I am always thinking about you and them
at home. I know it's no use doing that but they have always
behaved well to me that's the reason I can't forget.

We dear Sister I don't think I have got any more new to tell
you. I hope you went to Joanna's wedding, I wish her good luck.
Well dear now I must close hoping this will find you quite well. With
my best love and good wishes to you, from your loving Brother,

Arthur

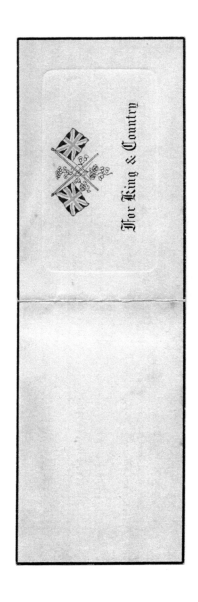

In Loving Memory
— of —

ARTHUR WILLIAM,

The dearly beloved and eldest son of ALBAN & ANNE HATCHER,

BLYTHBURGH,

**Who was killed in action on September 4th, 1916,
at Fallemont Farm, near Guillemont,**

Aged 19 Years.

A sudden change, at God's command he fell,
He had no time to bid his friends farewell;
Death came without a warning given,
We hope at last to meet in heaven.

The blow is bitter the loss severe
To part with one we loved so dear,
It was God's will it should be so,
At his command we all must go.

We little thought when he left home,
That death so soon would be his doom,
But it is true what the Scripture saith,
"In the midst of life we are in death."

THE INSTITUTE OF DEMOLITION ENGINEERS

This is to certify that

A.G. Clarke

was elected a Fellow of

THE INSTITUTE OF DEMOLITION ENGINEERS

on the twenty-ninth *day of* October 1993

Witness our hands and Seal at London this

twenty-ninth *day of* October 1993

President

Secretary

EⁱᴵR

The Lord Chamberlain is
commanded by Her Majesty to invite

Mr. and Mrs. A. G. Clarke

to a Garden Party
at Buckingham Palace
on Tuesday, 22nd July 2003 from 4 to 6 pm

This card does not admit

Our invitation to Buckingham Palace

HISTORICAL FACTS CONCERNING THE LIFE OF
ARTHUR GEORGE CLARKE

1922	Born at Blythburgh, Suffolk
1926	Attended Blythburgh Elementary School
1931	Attended Wenhaston Elementary School
1937	Left school and obtained work at The Empire Pool, Wembley (part of the Wembley Stadium complex).
1938	Returned to Suffolk. Worked for summer months as a Walls ice cream salesman.
1939	Signed on the steam drifter "Foresight" fishing from Lowestoft, moving round the coast of Fleetwood and fishing the Irish Sea until the drifter was commandeered by the Royal Navy to serve as Balloon Barrage outside the British ports.
1940	Signed on Prestatyn Rose, a coasting vessel until illness enforced my departure.
1941	Signed on "SS Mirupanu" as Able Seaman trading the east coast from London to Blyth. Remained on ship for two years.
1943	Signed on "SS Cherbourg" again trading on the east coast, later changing to another larger and better ship.

1943	Signed on the "MV Empire Ness" again trading on the east coast. The ship was commandeered by the War Office and was used as a supply vessel backing up the Normandy landings. Was at Arromanches on `D-Day' following up the troops until the ship was sunk in the Schelt en route for Ghent. Transferred to `SS Greta Force' for a short duration.
1944	Transferred to the "MV Kemball Harlow" again on special operations supplying the troops.
1945	Signed on "MV Royal Daffodil" ferrying troops from Continent to Dover. Was chosen to represent the Merchant Navy (one of four men) to parade in the Albert Hall at the Empire Festival of Youth.
1946	Obtained discharge from the Merchant Service to re-enter fishing industry - longshore fishing from Southwold Beach. Bad weather and lack of earnings forced a change of occupation and resulted in a short term as stoker at Southwold Gas Works before joining a gang of itinerant Irish workers on agricultural work.
1950	Became a Gang-master and employed 27 No. labourers on local farms carrying out all types of agricultural operations - mainly re-excavation of ditches and draining schemes. Later obtaining police permission to store and use explosives. Experience gained from trial and error, the facility opened up the opportunity to demolish War Department defence structures on the east coast and also a large defence system at West Point, Pembrokeshire.

1956	Formed a company known as Clarke Demolition and Construction Co. Ltd and also commence farming, in own right, by purchasing two farm at Hinton and Halesworth in Suffolk. The same year I commenced trading as a landscape and grounds maintenance contractor, securing many term maintenance contracts on MOD establishments throughout East Anglia and 6 British bases in Germany.
1960	The company obtained membership to the National Federation of Demolition Contractors and have since supported the Federation in every respect.
1985-87	I was elected Vice Chairman of the London & Southern Counties branch of the National Federation of Demolition Contractors.
1987-89	Was elected Chairman of the London and Southern Counties branch – serving for 2 years.
1989	Elected to serve on the National Council of the NFDC.
1993	Elected as a Fellow of the Institute of Demolition Engineers after serving for many years as a member.
1998	Now in retirement the original company has been re-organised as follows: **Clarke Development Corporation plc** CDC Demolition Ltd **Land & Leisure Group Ltd** CDC Landscapes Ltd Greensports Ltd Waldringfield Heath Golf Club Ltd

*Visit to Cobh in Ireland, the Black Watch called
there on the way back to the UK after the short
'D' Day voyage.
With an old friend and the Taxi driver visiting
the graves of the WW1 sinking of the Lusitania*

**For further information about this
or any of our publications, please
contact Martal Publications of Ipswich**

Customer Information Line 01473 720573
Email: martalbooks@msn.com

**Published and Printed
by
Martal Publications of Ipswich**
*PO Box 486
IPSWICH
United Kingdom
IP4 4ZU*